A

VIEW

FROM THE

BACK PEW

A
VIEW
FROM THE
BACK PEW

God, Religion & Our Personal Quest for Truth

TIM O'DONNELL

For information, address:

Linchpin Publishing LLC
P.O. Box 480256
Kansas City, MO 64148
E-mail: publisher@linchpinpublishing.com

For foreign and translation rights, contact Nigel J. Yorwerth.
E-mail: nigel@publishingcoaches.com.

Library of Congress Control Number: 2010905574

ISBN: 978-0-9845344-1-8

10 9 8 7 6 5 4 3 2 1

Cover design: Nita Ybarra
Interior design: Alan Barnett

Distributed by SCB Distributors

To those who have the courage
to ask the far-reaching questions

CONTENTS

Introduction   ix

1   DOCTRINE AND DOGMA   1
    Taking Mysteries on Faith

2   WHAT IS GOD?   17
    Infinite Intelligence and Our Ascending Urge

3   DISCUSSION AND DOUBT   33
    Looking for God in All the Wrong Places

4   WHAT IS RELIGION?   51
    Putting God on Paper

5   DISILLUSION AND DISCOVERY   71
    The University of Life

6   WHAT IS CHRISTIANITY?   85
    From Deposit to Doctrine

7   THE DEAL   103
    When in Rome . . .

8   WHAT IS THE TRINITY?   121
    The Math behind the Mystery

9   RISE AND FALL   131
    Down Payment on The Deal

10   **WHO ARE THE CLERGY?**   143
     Personnel "Matters"

11   **THE DEAL DELIVERS**   161
     God's End of the Bargain

12   **WHO IS JESUS?**   185
     Christ Consciousness and the Kingdom Within

13   **DISCERNING THE DIVINE**   211
     Out of the World and into the Woods

14   **PRACTICING ONENESS**   239
     The Conversation of Our Life

Epilogue   253

Acknowledgments   259

Notes   263

INTRODUCTION

Question (n). 1. A sentence worded or expressed so as to elicit information. 2. A doubt about the truth or validity of something. 3. The raising of an objection or a doubt.

Questions. Beautiful, fantastic, enlightening, and exciting! Questions. Without them, where would our species be today? Would we still be traveling in caravans? Would we still worship the beasts of the field? Would we accept the world to be as flat as our eye tells us it is?

When I was ten years old, a smart-aleck fifth grader in parochial school, I peppered my teachers with questions every chance I got. *Why do we have to eat fish sticks on Friday? What is a Blessed Virgin? If we're all God's children, why do you keep calling Jesus the only Son of God?* Three decades later, when I was a daily newspaper publisher at the height of my career, the questions had changed, but not my need to ask them. *Are spirituality and religion the same thing? Is guilt a necessary part of the religious experience? Do the rules of religion actually help me get closer to God?*

Asking questions is the quintessential human activity. It's what *makes* us human. We're programmed to want to know how things work, why the world is the way it is, where we came from, and why we're here. We approach these audacious questions from different angles—science, philosophy, theology—and while some of their adherents would disagree, I don't believe that any one discipline has a corner on the answers. Just as there are many tributaries to a river, there is more than one path to Truth.

I received the consummate Catholic education, attending Catholic grade school, high school, and college. Along the way I was pummeled by nuns, cajoled by priests, and humored by serious theologians as I tried to satisfy my nagging doubts about the religion of my birth and its role in my life. I was put off by what I perceived as the easy explanations of faith that the Catholic Church offered—and yet at a crucial point in my young life I experienced a connection with God that transcended everything I had been taught to believe. There was a contest taking place between my religious education and my spiritual inclination that left my soul's well-being hanging in the balance. And there it hung for years.

I was taught one thing but I was experiencing another. Experience is much more vigorous than belief, and I struggled mightily to square the two. It took half a lifetime to comprehend that all the time I'd been trying to make sense of religion, I had actually been feeling the presence in my life of the Being I'd been trained to call God; I just hadn't recognized Him.

Suddenly I faced a new question: *could my religion actually be obstructing my personal quest for Truth?*

I decided to find out which was true, my religious conditioning or my spiritual intuition. And I decided to do this by questioning *everything*—everything I was taught to believe and everything I sought to believe. I dove headfirst into the taboo questions of Christianity—the ones the nuns had taught us on pain of hellfire never to challenge—not as a theologian but as an investigative reporter, and I demanded the same objectivity from myself that I demanded from reporters.

I started with the biggest questions and worked inward, searching for the truth about man's relationship to God. I expected that my religious training would somehow make sense of my spiritual intuition, and I thought that my questions would lead me to an answer that was complete in and of itself. But as I closed in on the core of my questioning, I began to see that *what* I had learned and *how* I had learned it were inextricably intertwined.

A View from the Back Pew alternates some of the key episodes in my life with some of the answers I think I've discovered, tracing my search for balance between the dogma of Catholicism and a hunch about a more accessible spiritual presence in my life. This book is not the prodigious accumulation of integrated wisdom that might satisfy philosophers, theologians, and the spiritual illuminati. I have nothing to add to these people's understanding; I look to them to expand mine. Rather, I hope it is a first step for people like me to begin their *own* personal journeys from ritualized systems of belief to a more vital connection with the intelligence that animates the universe, the essence that we are trained to call God.

I wrote *A View from the Back Pew* for those of you who have pondered in your hearts the same questions I explore—about God, belief, doctrine, the role of organized religion, and the possibilities of personal spirituality. I know that the questions I tackle here are the same that many Christians carry from catechism into adulthood, even if they have never admitted it to others or even articulated them fully to themselves. Maybe you've never asked these questions out loud. Maybe you've asked without getting satisfactory answers. Or maybe you simply sense that there is something more to be grasped just beyond your reach, a piece of the puzzle that will leave you more fulfilled than you are now.

Asking questions is the way to extend your reach and grasp that missing piece. I'm troubled by reports of people declaring themselves agnostic and leaving their churches in droves. To me it's a kind of cop-out. I may not agree with the conclusion an atheist draws about God, but at least he has asked enough questions to draw a conclusion. It's all too common today for people who become disillusioned with their religion, frustrated with its dogma and ritual, to stop asking questions altogether. They just walk away—and inadvertently turn their backs on God as well.

I have written this book for those who spar with religion— in any form—and find themselves struggling with God. *Knowing religion is not necessarily the same as knowing God.* My hope is that if you are drawn to the Divine but labor over dogma, doctrine, and ritual, you may find support in my story and the possibility of a fresh perspective in my view from the back pew.

Here's hoping my tributary to the river of Truth helps you to discover your own.

ONE

DOCTRINE AND DOGMA

Taking Mysteries on Faith

A t Santa Maria del Popolo we went to confession every Friday. There was always anxiety amongst us boys as we waited to step into the box opposite Father Murphy. The girls had much less to fear because they didn't sin as much as we gross boys did; they didn't talk in class that much (a sin), they didn't lie to their moms as much (a sin), they never swore (another sin), and they hardly ever hit their little brothers (a very common sin). The girls were in a separate line, zipping in and out of the confessional, while our line nervously lingered, it seemed, for hours.

There was so much confession that it got repetitive. Sometimes we joked that we should "do stuff" just to have something new to tell the priest in the box. And there were no secrets in the pews; confessions and their corresponding penance were openly discussed. "Wudja do?" was the inevitable query while in line waiting to get into the box, "Wudja get?" while waiting after penance for everyone else to finish. A few Hail Marys and couple of Our Fathers were the norm, so when some knucklehead spent an unusual amount of time kneeling at the railing in front of the altar, we all knew

1

a serious offense—a "big" (mortal) sin—had been committed. Penances were compared, details shared, and stories embellished as we spent Friday mornings cleaning our souls for weekend Mass. Because, as we all knew, if you went to Communion on Sunday with a dirty soul, you would be in big trouble with God.

A SLICE OF AMERICAN PIE

Santa Maria del Popolo, or SMdP (So Many Dumb People, as we wisecracks called it), was in the heart of "uptown" Mundelein, Illinois, a white-flight haven of the early '60s named after George Cardinal Mundelein, Archbishop of Chicago from 1915 to 1939. Mundelein in the '60s was a quaint little hamlet where you could easily envision Wally and Beaver walking the tree-lined streets to school and back, happy and safe in an idyllic corner of a burgeoning suburbia—a perfectly portioned piece of American Pie. The tract housing looked as if the same builder had built every house; most houses were either boxy little ranches with three bedrooms or split-levels with the three bedrooms upstairs, kitchen, living room, and dining room on the ground floor, and a basement to boot. The streets were lined with saplings that would one day canopy the manicured quarter-acre square lots with shade and filled with kids on bikes zipping around in anticipation of their dads' return each evening from their jobs in Chicago. Mundelein's founders must have anticipated the invasion of thousands of kids, because public parks were central to city planning. There was at least one park, inclusive of ball diamonds, swing sets, sandboxes, merry-go-rounds, slides, and monkey bars, within walking distance of every subdivision in town. A kid in any neighborhood could go to a park without having to cross one of the two "busy" streets, which were Hawley and Lake.

The meticulously manicured Little League Field was Mundelein's pride and joy, as Little League Baseball was a collective preoccupation of the citizenry, who all seemed to have a hand in building it, maintaining it, manning concession stands, chalking fields, coaching, umpiring, or raising money. Summer evenings at the Little League Field was where you could catch up on the town scuttlebutt, see who had a new car, new job, or new hairdo, or hear whispers of who was in trouble at home. Mundelein also boasted nearly a dozen watering holes, most of them stretching along Lake Street from north to south with Santa Maria right in the midst of them all. Joints like Earl & Marge's, Emil's, The Chug-a-Lug, The Point, The Channel, The Do Drop Inn, and The Irish Mill were as much a part of the fabric of this suburban utopia as were the various civic groups like Saint Vincent DePaul, the Jaycees, or the Rotary. Mundelein was a hard-working, hard-drinking hamlet, a growing place and a place for growing. It was perfect in its imperfections, and a large portion of the town was Catholic.

Though both of my parents were raised as Catholics, ours was not a highly religious household. I have early memories of attending Mass every Sunday with my three brothers and my mom, returning home to the smell of bacon frying as my dad prepared a big Sunday breakfast for the family. As the years went by, Mass became less of a family ritual and more of an optional practice for any of us brothers who volunteered to attend. My parents' divorce when I was ten years old brought an end to many family customs, Sunday Mass and the big Sunday breakfast being just one. It wasn't until many years later that I learned of the disillusionment they each felt over the Catholic Church's position on their split. Meantime, they still insisted on a Catholic education for us, but our indoctrination was left largely to the Church, specifically the nuns at our parish school.

I spent the better part of eight years under the nuns' near-constant surveillance—a period I recall with near-equal parts sweet nostalgia and white-knuckle angst. The sisters of Santa Maria del Popolo were responsible for molding us into good little Catholics, and they took this responsibility very seriously. These Brides of Christ were nothing if not zealous about their mission, and they mesmerized and terrorized us, probably without any intention of doing either. The black veils and starched white wimples they wore as part of their habits pinched their faces into scowls that kept us in a state of apprehension sometimes verging on outright fear.

The parish was the center of suburban life in the '60s and growing up was a collaborative process. We attended class together, broke bread, played sports, and worshipped together, fought with each other and gossiped about each other, closely watched by the nuns all the while. The sisters tried to cultivate in their students love and respect for the Holy Roman Catholic Church, but often succeeded in cultivating a terror of all things Catholic instead. Their uncompromising obedience to the faith could be intolerant and at times unnerving. What they instilled in young Catholic minds has followed many into adulthood as a strange medley of devotion, foreboding, and shame.

BLACK EYES AND YARDSTICKS

Physically, I emerged from my schooling more or less unscathed. It was the fear of God, and the fear of nuns, that left the deepest impressions from my formative years in the Church. Nevertheless, some of my skirmishes with nuns were physically traumatic, and several resulted in minor facial contusions.

In first grade, while sitting in a little wooden chair, in formation as part of a reading group in front of the class, I first felt the sting of Catholicism. Sister James Denise was facing the rest of the class, while our little reading group was seated directly behind her against the front wall of the classroom. Someone in our group was talking, and of course Sister thought it was me (she was probably right), so without turning her head or missing a beat in her lesson, she deftly reached behind her and backhanded me square on the side of the face. She landed a powerful, clean knuckle-shot that left my cheek glowing crimson for the rest of the day. By the time I got home, I had the most magnificent battle scar a kid could wish for—my very first black eye. And I had learned a valuable lesson: watch where a nun hides her hands. When she wasn't using them to write on a chalkboard or to help her articulate finer points of our religious training, they were usually concealed within the folds of her penguinesque habit. I was leery of the camouflaged limbs from that point forward.

In third grade, I was the star of religion class one day when I answered a series of questions correctly, almost entirely by luck. I don't recall what the first question was, but something about Sister Mary Alice's cadence gave me a clue that the answer to the second question was the same answer I had given to the first, and then I gave the identical answer for the third as well. By my fourth correctly duplicated response, Sister was so excited by my theological prowess that she reached into her little paper box of stars and came rushing toward me with a gold one balanced on the end of her pudgy index finger. Filled with delight, she took aim at my forehead. In anticipation of the praise about to be heaped on me, either I twitched or she misfired—but either way, Sister thrust that star-spangled pointer toward me only to miss my forehead and plunge it directly into my socket. My eye watered all day and, even though earned in a quite different manner, a black eye would be my prize on this day as well.

In fifth grade, Sister Ilene Marie (aka Prune) had occasion to wield her yardstick, which was usually little more than an idle threat, against my outstretched left hand. She swung and missed. Maybe I had moved a little, maybe she just had bad aim, but she was furious—and because I laughed at her whiff, she instructed me to put my hand atop my desk so she could have a stationary target. She brought the yardstick down with such force on my hand that she broke her trusty weapon in two. Now she was really mad, maybe because I snickered again, maybe because her beloved three-foot instrument of justice was broken, and she collected both pieces of the yardstick, stacked them together to form a shorter but much more substantial saber, and hit me again. This time she whacked me a good one. There was nothing funny anymore, this one really hurt, but I still laughed, probably so I wouldn't cry. By now the boys in the class were howling, the girls were gasping, Sister Ilene was mad as a hornet, and her hand surprised everyone as it crashed against the side of my head. The whole class was stunned, including Sister Ilene. This was far more physically violent than she was known to be; she was a sweet, frail, elderly lady with an Irish brogue who wasn't prone to administering corporal punishment, but was normally quite tender with us, the threatening yardstick notwithstanding. Now we were both in tears, and the result—you guessed it, a shiner once again.

One evening in sixth grade I knew a call was coming home from Sister Mary Alice (her again) about my constant clowning in class and general lackluster performance. I sat at the desk in my bedroom, feigning scholastic diligence in a ridiculous attempt to mollify my mother when the call inevitably came. Finally, at about 7:00, the phone rang and it was Sarge, as we called her by then. I could overhear my mom's end of the conversation and I could tell Sarge was getting her worked up pretty good. As I sat and waited for the call to end, I was getting very nervous. Then I heard the phone slam down and my mom's angry foot-stomps marching toward my room. I bent closer to the book in front of me to emphasize my studiousness, my body rigid with dread and my face mere inches from my desk. My mom rapped me on the back of the head and the bridge of my nose crashed into the 90-degree edge. I saw blood drip onto the book in front of me. From a very small cut on the bridge of my nose, blood was flowing down both sides into my mouth. I flung my head back and the blood ran crossways under my eyes toward my ears. By the time I turned around to face my mom, I had blood running all down and across my face. It looked a lot worse than it was, and she was horrified. Within minutes, she was on the phone cursing the nun who provoked her to take such an action. I was no longer the target of her ire—Sarge was—but guess what? Another mouse for me, this time a double.

DEBATABLE DOCTRINE

At Santa Maria del Popolo, a nuanced appreciation of Roman Catholic theological thought was not the nuns' agenda. We were fed an uncompromising message built on a few key points. God lived up in the sky, beyond the stars, in a place called Heaven, where the faithful were called to join him when they died. If we died with the stain of sin on our souls, we were punished by being sent to a different place, below the surface of the earth, called Hell, where we would suffer in flames for eternity. In between the two there was a place called Purgatory where some sinners could do penance in order to get into Heaven, which, by the way, was only for baptized Catholics. A baby who died before being baptized would go to yet a fourth place, called Limbo—forever! It hardly seemed fair.

Most important, we were all born into a state of sin that separated us from God, because of the "original sin" of Adam and Eve. I wasn't quite clear on what that sin had been, but I knew what it meant: God was disappointed in us from the very start.

It was so bad that God had to send His son to earth to make up for it. He caused a virgin by the name of Mary to become pregnant with this son, whose name was Jesus. Mary learned of her pregnancy from a visiting angel. Joseph, Mary's husband, went along with this plan willingly. Mary remained a virgin her entire life.

Jesus was born in a stable on the first Christmas Eve. He started a church—our church, the Holy Roman Catholic Church—but then he was killed by the Jews. (I didn't know what Jews were, but they must be pretty bad people if they killed Jesus.) Jesus rose from the dead three days after the Jews killed him, on the first Easter morning. He did all this to "pay" for the original sin on our souls. But we still had to tell our sins to a priest in a box behind a screen so that God would forgive us and not punish us for eternity.

None of these points were supposed to be debatable, but I managed to debate them anyway. I wasn't the best student at Santa Maria and I wasn't the worst, but one class I always took an interest in was religion. There was something intriguing to me about the rituals and mysteries of the Catholic Church—something thought-provoking but not completely satisfying, incongruent to a budding inquisitive instinct. I detected a subtle hypocrisy even as a youngster, though I wouldn't have known to call it that. So when the nuns weren't pummeling me, I was goading them with an ongoing, antagonistic, quasi-academic, smart-ass-oriented cross-examination. I was innately suspicious of sanctimonious explanations to my questions that resorted to a "mystery of faith" as an answer. I didn't like it when I felt I had a teacher cornered and she stifled me with "It's a mystery of faith." To me, these mys-

teries were what they used when they ran out of logical explanations. We weren't supposed to keep questioning once a "mystery" was invoked; it displayed a lack of faith, and that was not
to be tolerated. I felt frustrated whenever I wheedled this answer
from a nun—but also a little triumphant. They definitely didn't
like the smarmy schoolboy smugness that expressed itself in such
moments, and they took it out on me on my report card and in
parent conferences by reporting I was disrespectful and "talked
back too much."

One mystery of faith in particular presented me with a challenge: Mary, the mother of Jesus. Mary looms large for Catholics
and the lore surrounding her is vast. The challenge was in understanding her place in the big picture of the religion. Catholics
worship Mary with a deistic reverence; by calling her the Mother
of God and making her the matriarch of the Holy Family, the
theology seems to position her on a level with God. At Santa Maria,
we were taught to pray to Mary as we were taught to pray to God.
My own mother prayed directly to Mary exclusively, on the theory
that if anyone could get God to do something, it was God's own
mother. With four sons, she believed the mother was the most
influential character in any man's life, even God's.

But the theology also teaches that God was the father of Jesus
while Mary was Jesus' mother. So I continually harangued the nuns
on these points. Was Mary like God? Was she Jesus' mother and
God's mother too, or just Jesus'? Where did Joseph fit in? What
does "Blessed Virgin" mean? What is a virgin, anyway? (Later,
when I knew, I feigned ignorance so I could continue to hound
the nuns.) Mary was one of the mysteries I simply would not give
the nuns a pass on.

As the namesake of our parish (named for Saint Mary of the
People, a church in Rome), Mary had a special, shady grotto of

her own on the grounds between the convent and the playground. Every May we had the biggest event in our school calendar, May Crowning, a holy and moving tribute to "the Queen of Heaven and the Mother of God." (See what I mean?) The entire school practiced for this solemn ceremony, starting in January. Each of the eight grades had its own role to play, and a pair of eighth graders was selected, one boy and one girl, to place a crown of flowers on the life-sized statue. On the grotto's perfectly manicured patch of green lined with spring flowers, the entire student body assembled, from the smallest first graders in the front to the big kids from the eighth grade in back, to watch the chosen two carry a beautiful handmade crown of flowers down an aisle of grass to the Queen.

For some reason, this ceremony made me cry real tears. Every year from first grade to eighth, I wept at May Crowning. There was one song in particular, *Immaculate Mary*, which invariably turned on the waterworks. I had no idea why, and to this day I'm not quite sure. But I've sometimes wondered if my challenges to the mystery of Mary were the reason I cried so profusely at the annual ceremony in her honor. Did I feel guilty about questioning the very essence of the Mother of God? Did I feel Mary's disappointment in me for making wisecracks at her expense? Was it my way of showing remorse? Catholics have a strange yet intimate relationship with guilt, and I guess I felt it every May for eight years.

FALLING CRUMBS OF JESUS

I might have resisted the "mysteries of faith" the nuns tried to pass off as truth, but I found comfort in the ritual of the Mass. The structure of the liturgy, the familiar melodic patterns of music, even the pungency of the incense was reassuring and familiar, and when I was old enough to become an altar boy, I gained a sense of responsibility and an air of prominence. I loved the pomp and circumstance that ranged from the pre-Mass preparations in the sacristy—lighting the candles, preparing the wine and the water, helping the priest put on his vestments—to the big show on the altar of the main church, with the little box on it called the tabernacle, where God lived.

Every Sunday I was "on stage" with the priest in front of my peers, their parents, and other Catholics of Mundelein, assisting in administering the word of God as I performed the important task of opening the big book to the assigned passage and then holding it during readings, lectern-like, before Monsignor Meaghan or one of the priests who served under him. There was mystery at work here too: the nuns taught us that what happened when the bread and wine were turned into the body and blood of Christ was an actual, not a symbolic, transformation. It could only be done by a Catholic priest. But I played an important role as I rang the bell three times at precisely the right moment and held a brass dish under every chin receiving Holy Communion to catch any falling crumbs of Jesus; the Mass couldn't be conducted without me. After Mass I extinguished the candles and cleaned up the altar. This was important and pious work. I also enjoyed the boys-only aspect of the role. The girls, though they seemed to be favored by the nuns in the classroom during the week, were not eligible for this holy tour of duty.

I loved being part of the big show on Sundays in the main church. Weekday Mass at 7 a.m. was a different story. This Mass lasted only about 20 minutes for the eight or ten regulars who attended, and it was celebrated in the much less glamorous outpost of the "little chapel" across the street from the main church. It was here that I noticed a different type of worshiper, a different type of service, indeed a different kind of Catholicism. There was no music or pomp here, just a reading from the Old Testament and one from the New, then the Gospel—no homily—and finally the distribution of the Sacrament. The few who came to Mass on weekdays were clearly there to get Communion and little else mattered.

At first I thought they were merely going through the motions of Mass; cold, efficient, and impersonal were the order of these gatherings, anything but passionate or inspiring. But gradually I began to realize that in this small group of regulars were the truly faithful of the parish. There was no need for fancy Sunday clothing, ceremony, song or show, just the Eucharist. These devout people needed only to pray within the quiet of their own private space. They practiced their faith for themselves, not for the benefit of the congregation. In fact, after a while, these Catholics made me look a bit differently at the Sunday crowd.

FAITH AND FEAR

At the end of eighth grade, I would leave grade school and enter the Catholic high school in Mundelein. As the time neared, I looked forward to trading in the nuns of Santa Maria for the priests of Carmel High School, even though the nuns browbeat us with stories about how the priests thrashed and beat the Carmel boys. We were like young recruits going off to boot camp, ready for whatever those tough old priests had in store for us, ready to be forged into Catholic men—but mostly we were ready to get away from Sarge and Prune and the gang of nuns who'd dogged us for eight years about what disappointing Catholics we were turning out to be.

I understand now that it is quite possible the nuns knew much more about spiritual development than they shared with us schoolchildren. Maybe they did have more to offer than the rote of catechism and the wrath of God, but doubted they could reach young minds with deeper theology. Or maybe they were instructed to keep us focused on fear of God and strict adherence to ritual. I don't believe, as I may have at one time, that they were frustrated, mean women who had a warped view of God and took joy in bedeviling me. For the most part, the nuns involved in my life were well-intentioned people caught in the brackish waters of the post–Vatican II sea of change. They'd been taught a different brand of Catholicism than the one they were charged with teaching us, and the tension led plenty of pupils (like me) into confusion and recalcitrance about an angry, punishing God and his earthbound institution. The nuns were funny yet scary; mean yet compassionate; kind and angry and calm and neurotic. They were pudgy little caricatures of Catholicism who were central to our existence at a time, in an America, that was different than today. And I do have fond memories in spite of the fear.

But mostly, fear prevailed. I was afraid of Hell, I was afraid of yardsticks, and I was afraid of nuns. The lessons they taught led me to feel God was remote and angry—especially with me. The Church they represented was severe and unfriendly to any spiritual inclinations I might have had. Looking back, I think I did possess a propensity for spiritual inquiry and growth, but I was too mired in trying to memorize the rituals of the institution and avoid the wrath of God to allow these natural tendencies to emerge. When they did, much later, I would search for answers about the Church and far beyond—and I would see that many of my questions grew out of the separation from God that we'd been taught was the defining condition of our souls. At the time, though, my response was often just to rebel against the sisters of Santa Maria.

Even so, I was at home in the Church then. I felt that as long as I participated in the rituals, I had a chance to go to Heaven.

As long as I memorized the doctrine and did good deeds, I just might escape the wrath of an always-angry God.

Leaving the nest of Santa Maria del Popolo and entering adolescence, this is what I believed:

- Because of Adam and Eve, we were all born into a state of "original sin." This state separated us from God.

- God lived in His kingdom in Heaven, which was a real place up in the sky. Hell, Purgatory, and Limbo were real places, too, but places we hoped not to go.

- Our job was to try to do what God wanted so He would not be angry with us. When we went wrong (which we always did), we had to confess our sins to a priest to be forgiven. Otherwise God would remember our infractions and punish us for eternity.

- God's son, Jesus, was born in a stable. His mother was a virgin named Mary. He came to earth to "pay" for the stain of original sin on our souls and to open the gates of Heaven, which were closed until then.

- Jesus started a church, the Catholic Church, which was the only way to Heaven. My best friend, Perry, who lived next door and attended the Community Church, would never join me in Heaven unless he became a Catholic. (This tormented me immensely.)

- Someday, after we died, we would be reunited with our bodies. This was Judgment Day, when Jesus would return to "judge the living and the dead." The decision about our eternal fate would be made at that time.

- "I am not worthy." I didn't exactly know what this meant, but it must be important because we repeated it three times at every Mass.

This is an oversimplification of Catholic theology, of course, but it was the foundation given us by the nuns. It was what we were armed to enter the world with. The underlying message that disturbed me for many years was the steady message of alienation from God. There was no way around it because I was born a sinner and God punished sinners. Of course, I couldn't verbalize this problem of separation, or duality, at the time. Rather, I left the care of the nuns with a feeling that I was not worthy to communicate with God directly, but that I must talk to God through the Church, and I really didn't like the Church all that much.

I believed God existed, but I was afraid of Him. I felt God was always mad at me, forever disappointed in my many shortcomings. I was certain of my eternity spent in the tortures of Hell. From the perspective of my earliest indoctrination, religion seemed iron-fisted and eternity looked ominous.

TWO

WHAT IS GOD?

INFINITE INTELLIGENCE AND
OUR ASCENDING URGE

We know more than we did two thousand years ago. From the time of Jesus to the time of da Vinci, about fifteen hundred years later, scholars estimate that we humans doubled our knowledge. We doubled it again by the time the United States was born, less than three hundred years after that. By 1900, a little more than a hundred years later, our knowledge had once again doubled, and fifty years later, by 1950, it had doubled again. From 1950 to 1960, a mere decade, the total body of human knowledge doubled yet again. It is estimated that our knowledge now doubles every 18 months or so.

We humans are pretty amazing creatures when it comes to knowing stuff.

From the earliest human history, we have been responding to our inborn need for knowledge. Our overpowering curiosity demands that we gather knowledge about the physical world that surrounds us, and it also propels a yearning to know and understand what may exist beyond the physical—the *metaphysical*. What drives this continuing quest?

From the macro, or collective, point of view, the driving questions address world events and the outcomes of world affairs as a whole. *What is the origin of the human race? What are the facts of our present condition? What is our destiny?*

From the micro, or individual, point of view, the questions are similar but much more personal: *Where did I come from? Where am I going? What is my purpose?*

This urge to look beyond our natural, physical experience to understand the meaning and purpose of our own life reverberates to us from our earliest ancestors. It initiates the call that echoes in the deepest recesses of our own mind and sends us in search of connection with something greater than ourselves. From the earliest human history there exists evidence of human piety, the seemingly natural tendency for us to be reverent—*to worship something*. The earliest signs of worship come from Australian Aboriginals about sixty thousand years ago, but there is ample evidence that systems of belief incorporating metaphysical or supernatural entities—deities—have been with us in one form or another for as long as we've been walking upright. The tendency to "believe" in something seems to be written in human DNA.

I call this inclination our *Ascending Urge.*

It is estimated that the universe is between 14 and 15 *billion* years old and Earth is 4.5 billion years old. Mankind, or *Homo sapiens,* in its present state of physical evolution has been around for about one hundred thirty thousand years, just a fraction of that time. We humans are relative newcomers to the cosmic order, so for those first creatures endowed with self-awareness, our ancestors, to have instinctively sensed power, intelligence, and order beyond their own seems completely reasonable and perfectly plausible. For us, these many millennia later, to continue the pursuit of this same Universal Intelligence seems reasonable as well.

If the universe did not have a tendency to favor continuation of itself, then surely there would be more chaos in the cosmos than order. The very fact that Earth has not been obliterated by haphazard collision with another planet or solar system suggests that continuation is by design. For Earth *not* to collide with something in 4.5 billion years thanks to cosmic coincidence is not reasonable to believe; some Intelligence must be keeping chaos at bay.

To Frank Sheed, a Catholic writer, belief in a guiding Intelligence is not a matter of sanctity as much as it is a matter of sanity. "To overlook God's presence," he writes, "is not simply to be irreligious; it is a kind of insanity, like overlooking anything else that is actually there."[1] He likens it to seeing a coat hanging on a wall and not realizing it is being held up by a hook, but rather believing it exists in a fantastical world in which coats ignore gravity and adhere to walls by a power of their own. To fail to see a Universal Intelligence "holding up" the universe, one would have to be living in an equally fantastic world. For Sheed, the evidence of God's existence is obvious even if God isn't visible to man.

As we start to inquire into the Infinite Intelligence at work in our world, our Ascending Urge leads us to its own set of primal questions.

Is God a reality? An idea?

Did God create man? Did man invent God?

What does God look like, what is His nature, and what do we call Him?

Is there one God? Are there many?

Is there a God who lives in the desert, another who
lives in Mecca, a third who lives in Rome?

Can we prove that God exists?

Why do we believe in the first place?

Answering these questions for oneself is a matter of individual credo or perhaps a matter of indoctrination. You believe, don't believe, or don't know. What you conclude about divine presence is your *personal theology,* and everyone has one. Whether you adopt a prepackaged system of beliefs in the form of a religion, experience a particular personal revelation, or are a nonbeliever, you have a theology about the Divine. In some way, to some degree, we are all theologians.

THE LONG VIEW

Several years ago, I sat on a plateau high above Sedona, Arizona, gazing out over the rose-colored desert that once had been the floor of an ancient ocean. I could see for miles into the distance, and from where I sat, there seemed to be no horizon, just an endless vista of carved red rock. I had the sense, too, that I was looking back millions of years over the landscape of time: I could see the stratified lines of age on the vertical cliffs, and with just a little imagination I could envision the deeply cut canyons and valleys filled with water and populated by frolicking ocean life the size of 747s. What great conspiracy had created this panorama of beauty that sat so perfectly motionless yet was so obviously vital and alive?

As I breathed in the beauty of the earthscape, I saw it change before my eyes. The red rocks of Sedona seemed to be changing color and hue as the sun changed angles, with me as the solitary witness. And even as I saw the time passing because of the play of light, I also felt time come to a complete standstill. I felt connected in a very material way to everything I saw. I was certain I could step off the cliff and land on the next plateau, which must have been miles away. After what seemed like a couple of seconds but was really a couple of hours, my mind fixated on the concept of *infinity* and wouldn't let go. It was here, ruminating on the idea of infinity, that I felt my entire mindset about God begin to shift.

I understood without the limitation of labels, without the use of words, that God was bigger than big, larger than the endless-seeming vista before me, yet small enough to reside within all that I saw. And I realized—the first time I'd done so in any real way—that God could only be *pure spirit*. This would not be the end of my expanding understanding of God, but it was certainly a new beginning: I was beginning to understand what I had failed to understand throughout my life. I was getting an inkling of some new knowledge that would confirm every challenge I'd ever raised to my religious education and lay the foundation for a new and deeper comprehension of God. Of course this was merely a seed of knowledge; it would need much care and feeding, but I sensed the seed was sown and I was on my way to understanding more about the Truth I had been seeking ever since I was a smart-ass kid hassling nuns.

WHAT WE BELIEVE

Broadly speaking, people fall into one of the following categories: theists, who believe in a deity whether or not its existence can be proven; atheists, who believe no supreme being exists because it can't be proven; and agnostics, who believe we cannot know for sure if a deity exists or not. Most of us have been agnostic at some point in our lives, even if it was for one day or one moment or because of a singular event. It is quite normal, quite human in fact, not to know for sure. If faith in God were universally easy for mankind, it would not be faith. By definition, faith requires a belief in something unseen and unproven; this isn't always easy. Rare is the person who has *never* questioned God's existence.

Among those who do believe, many consider that an infinite being created the universe and has an active and ongoing interest in the outcome of our collective and individual experience. Others believe such a being is responsible for creating the universe but not otherwise active in human affairs. Some believe that a Creator was the First Cause and set the universe in motion, while others believe each part of creation was created separately (in six days). These people are all theists. Most, though not all, theists "belong" or adhere to a belief system called a "religion" that offers orientation on doctrine and practice. The religion is intended to be the path that leads adherents to union with the Divine.

It's easy to get mired in "isms" when we talk about the multitude of beliefs mankind holds about God. In general terms, most of today's religions of the world are monotheistic (one god) as opposed to polytheistic (several gods), and yet polytheism came first. Most primitive civilizations believed that forces in the natural world were deities: the sun, the wind, the ocean, various animals, and so on. As humanity evolved in awareness and increased its capacity to understand, cultures throughout the world advanced toward the concept of a singular god. Spiritual teacher Ernest Holmes wrote in his classic *The Science of Mind,* "Man's idea of Deity evolves with his other ideas. After belief in many gods, he comes to realize there is One Mind and One Spirit back of all manifestation."[2] Our Ascending Urge to commune with entities greater than ourselves began with worshipping animal life, progressed to forces of nature, moved on to a pantheon of gods responsible for different aspects of human life, and finally evolved into an understanding of one infinite and omnipotent spiritual being with dominion over the universe.

Most belief systems do embrace other, secondary or lesser spiritual beings in addition to God that have an interest in affecting our natural life, such as saints, angels, demons, or avatars. These beings are attendants to God, protectors of mankind, and intercessors between the two; they are generally seen as spiritually greater than humans but lesser than God. What I find interesting about this shared belief is that it suggests that humans, throughout history, have interacted in some depth with the spirit world. How else could vast and intricate theologies be contrived and developed apart from one another yet contain such common ground? Either mankind has a universal desire that such beings exist or they *do* exist, be it in reality or in human collective consciousness.

But a belief in angels and demons doesn't undermine the supremacy of one singular deity or divert our natural evolution toward monotheism. Mankind's vote is in, and the consensus is that a singular, omnipotent, omniscient, and generally benevolent being exists; most concur that this being somehow caused the universe to be and to some degree has dominion over it. We may not all agree on this being's name, residence, or level of involvement in the natural world, or on how to commune with it, but the disagreements are not nearly as substantial as the various belief systems, past and present, would have us believe.

GOD IN OUR IMAGE

Many believers have a mental image of the Supreme Being. Typically, especially in the Judeo-Christian tradition, the image is of a "venerable man with a beard," as Frank Sheed puts it. August and authoritative, not particularly benevolent or compassionate, He is an imposing figure and one who instills a degree of fear. That's certainly how he looked in my imagination when I was waiting for my turn in the confessional at Santa Maria del Popolo. Depending on your frame of reference, He may look something like Karl Marx or possibly Gandalf. He is the God of the Sistine Chapel, bestowing His life force upon man, newly created "in His own image" with the mere touch of His finger.

Most schoolchildren in the West are indoctrinated with the image of the venerable old man, as I was, and this image can last a lifetime, even for those who intellectually come to understand the essence of God in a different way. God is the infinite unmanifest reality that manifests all that is in the physical universe, the nonphysical Being that brings all of reality into being and holds it there through intention, or awareness, of that which He has created. But the human mind thinks in pictures, and to visualize the infinite is a near impossibility. Most humans hold a mental image of God because it is human to do so.

For the same human reason, belief systems in all parts of the globe give names to God: Yahweh, Elohim, Allah, Bhagavan, Krishna, the Light, Jesus, Lord, Father, the Great Spirit, Brahman, Jehovah, or simply I Am. And because we have this inclination to personalize God, we often use the pronoun *He*, which suggests not only the essence and appearance of a human person but a gender as well. In fact, neither bodily form nor gender actually applies to God. Infinite Intelligence is a being, but one without form. God is not a person in the way we ordinarily think of a "person"; that is, God doesn't have structure, form, or shape. The Creator has intention and awareness, intelligence and purpose, but not a physical container that holds it. Every form in creation is imbued with some degree of this Infinite Spirit, but Spirit has no form per se.

When we speak of the Infinite Intelligence that we call God, we run up against the inadequacy of words to express pure spiritual essence. Since God is not an inanimate object, the word *it* is not accurate, yet the pronouns *he* and *she* suggest gender and so they are not accurate either. Human language is not suitable to express Divine Truth, but it's the only mechanism we have. So when I use the word *He*, I am not suggesting that God is a male entity. Despite the prevalent imagery of the venerable man with a beard, God is neither male nor female. Both male and female in the natural world are manifestations of the same Divine Spirit; both come from the same source of life. Pure spirit has no physical appearance other than that which it manifests through creation. So, while God looks like nothing, God at the same time looks like everything God creates.

THE INFINITY OF ETERNITY

To see past the teachings of duality (God up there, us down here) and gain a better sense of God's true spiritual essence, it's a good idea to spend a little time contemplating the meaning of infinity; this helps us to get past our simplistic picture of God with a gender and a name. Infinity is a slippery concept, so rather than grasping it tighter, we can try to let it come to us. When I sat in silent stillness high above the Arizona desert, infinity whispered to me to look closer, inviting me to simply receive the meaning of it and not try to decipher or to label what I was seeing. I wasn't going to *figure out* infinity; I could only accept it as the reality that it is.

We think of infinity as big. Really big! In fact, infinity is something else altogether: farther than any distance, larger than any measurement, and beyond any boundary. Infinity is an amount that can't be counted, a space that can't be measured. It has no boundary; it is never-ending.

If we look into the sky on a clear night, we can see the light from stars that are millions of light years away. They are all physical, manifest forms contained within the vastness of space. The stars and the space that contains them, including the galaxies swirling around them and the space in between those galaxies, are all contained within infinite space—or, more accurately, within the Creator of the space. The expansion of the universe could never surpass that which creates it. The Creator doesn't contract to meet creation; creation is constantly expanding (and evolving) in an attempt to meet the Creator.

Infinity—that is, God—is immeasurable. It extends outward in all directions forever. But that's only the big picture.

Infinity "extends" in the opposite direction as well. If the Creator exists throughout and beyond "outer" space, He also exists throughout "inner" space. Science has proven that all matter, even the densest rock, is made of individual and separate particles of matter. Through high-powered microscopes, we can see the separate particles within matter as well as the space between them. What appears to be solid contains *space* between its particles. Matter is actually the tiniest of particles moving so rapidly and randomly in open space that the movement gives an appearance of being solid, as Einstein's Kinetic Theory of Matter postulates.

If Spirit exists everywhere in outer "space," It is everywhere in matter as well, because within matter there exists the same "space" that exists between the stars. Some matter is denser and some is less dense. Solids are denser than liquid, liquids denser than gases. A human being is actually more open space than particles of matter. Man is not very dense at all, at least not when compared to a rock.

If we understand this space, this infinite ethereal substance that exists within, between and around all objects, to be Spirit, then to say that God dwells within us is not merely a figure of speech. Literally, Spirit is the energy that keeps *our* particles moving. Whatever name we give it—Spirit, Awareness, Infinite Intelligence—God is the actual medium that keeps us intact, the very life force of our existence.

If God were anything other than pure Spirit, His infiniteness would not be possible. If God had any physical part, that physical part would have to have been created, and that would make God part of creation. But since God is the Creator of all, He can't be contained within His own creation. He is beyond; He is bigger than the whole manifest creation that is the universe. If there were any element of the Infinite Intelligence that was not Spirit, it would not be infinite.

There's another implication to this concept of infinity. If there is one infinite being, then there cannot be another as well. If there were two beings considered infinite, one would contain or overlap the other and render it something other than infinite. Where would one infinite being begin and the other end?

The Infinite One can't be contained by space—but what about time? The Supreme Consciousness that is God exists beyond the limits of space as well as beyond the limits of time. God exists in eternity, which is defined not as endlessness but as timelessness. Time doesn't exist in eternity.

How do we get a grip on *that* slippery concept?

For a while, before I lost my taste for it, I was an efficient hunter. I could sit for hours and hours in a tree stand in the woods of eastern Kansas. When I first started hunting, I was completely out of sync with the rhythms of nature. I fidgeted almost nonstop, always moving, twitching and twisting to try and get comfortable.

My mind was constantly asking and answering questions, trying to label everything I saw. *What kind of flower is that? Why did that squirrel just do that? What kind of tree is that? What was that noise I just heard? Where is that bird flying off to?* And the most recurring question of all: *What time is it?* But in time—so to speak—I settled into silence and stillness. In that stillness, totally aware of my surroundings yet totally oblivious to the passing of minutes and hours, I found a sense of timelessness too—a glimpse of eternity.

It was only a glimpse, because that's all we are wired for. A human being is an individual point of consciousness that originates from Infinite Consciousness, and because our consciousness is limited (not infinite), we must experience time in linear fashion, one moment followed by another. We are able to distinguish past from present and present from future, but we can't experience them all at once. Our mind allows us to travel to the past via our memory, or into the future via anticipation of events to come, but we live in the eternal present; to human consciousness, it is always "now." The Infinite Awareness that is God experiences all that is throughout space and time, all at once. There is no past, present, or future in eternity.

ALL-SEEING, ALL-KNOWING

We've established that Spirit—God, the Creator, the Infinite One, Allah, or whatever name we bestow upon "Him"—is infinite and eternal. He possesses infinite intelligence as well. Spirit is *omniscient.* Just as God is not limited by having physical parts, His knowingness is not limited by learning.

There is nothing in the universe that becomes known at one point in time that is not already known by God in eternity. There isn't anything He doesn't know, there are no secrets, knowledge, or information withheld or hidden from Him; he "discovers" nothing. If one person in creation knows anything, the Infinite One already knows it. Any idea, invention, work of art, or discovery comes to the inventor, artist, or scientist by way of God's knowingness. Mankind can only discover what is already known by the Creator through the connection in consciousness to Him. Our knowledge unfolds throughout time, both collectively and individually; the Creator's knowingness is for all time. Mankind never has had a truly original thought.

When a scientist uncovers something new about nature, God already knows it, and that scientist is just tapping into the complete awareness God has of His own creation. The scientist is using the part of God's universal awareness that is the scientist's own individualized awareness. When an artist creates a masterpiece, he is connecting his inborn and individual creativity to God's universal and completely creative nature.

The Infinite Spirit created the entire universe, and there is nothing in the universe that is not under its dominion. When I say "created the universe," I am not contending that God created exactly as depicted in Genesis. "Created" could also mean "caused." *How* God created is not for us to know or understand; *that* He created is. God can effect any result within the universe without resistance. His willing any event is enough for it to happen. "Miracles" happen because the all-powerful nature of God is effecting an outcome that goes beyond human comprehension or beyond any capability known in the natural universe. God's power is *super*natural, beyond explanation or calculation.

As we'll see later, some people believe that Spirit is personal and engaged in the life of a man and the history of mankind, and some believe that God is impersonal and not engaged in our realm. Not all religious belief systems agree about Spirit's actual involvement in the natural world, but these disagreements are more about the will to be involved than about the capacity to be.

Because Spirit is both eternal and infinite, we can yet again conclude that there can only be one God. If Infinite Intelligence were lacking in some respect, there might be a need for some other entity to compensate for the lack. But to consider any lack is to consider something other than infinity. This is not to suggest that it is impossible to consider other spiritual beings, just the impossibility of more than one infinite being. An infinite being *must* be a spiritual one but a spiritual being is *not* necessarily an infinite one.

We have seen that mankind has a primal desire to communicate with the higher powers behind the mysteries of existence—a desire I call mankind's *Ascending Urge*. We have evolved in our understanding from simply worshipping things in the natural world that we don't understand, to submitting ourselves to the whims of a pantheon of gods who control our fate, to a mostly monotheistic understanding of a spiritual Being who created the universe and may participate actively in our life both individually and collectively. The concept of a singular deity is expressed in various ways throughout the world today, each developed contemporaneously according to culture and custom.

So, where does this leave us in our consideration of the Divine?

Part of being human is to possess the power of reason and the free will to use it, but we must not ignore the part of us that is purely Spirit in the process. Submitting rational thought to a review of the heart often creates a visceral feeling that is beyond reason: this is inspiration. Utilizing all of the capacity we are endowed with brings us closer to the Divine because we are moving toward the infinite state of Divine Awareness. We can be a mathematician *and* a mystic if we don't limit our conscious awareness to our rationality, or conversely, only to our heart. We can fuse the rationale with the visceral to create a state of awareness that can only be described as inspired. Doing so is being fully human.

So, before reading the next chapter, ponder infinity, reflect on eternity, consider monotheism as a possible conclusion to be drawn from it. Don't *accept* monotheism; *discover* it for yourself. Does it resonate with you? Is there something different that rings true? Does a council of gods feel right? Does God as pure Spirit make sense? Does it feel natural? Do your mind and your heart agree on the concept?

What I'm encouraging you to do is to follow *your own* Ascending Urge. Find a comfortable place to sit and close your eyes. (It doesn't need to be in Sedona.) Just let the word *infinity* settle in your mind. Then allow your understanding of it to rise within your thoughts. Don't worry if your mind wanders; just gently keep refocusing and see what happens. If you can do this outdoors, I suggest you *don't* close your eyes, but consider the vastness of the sky instead. You'll be surprised to see what rises as you meditate on infinity while filling your vision with it. Once you have an idea of what God means to you, you have the foundation for realizing your "personal theology."

THREE

DISCUSSION
AND DOUBT

Looking for God in
All the Wrong Places

Carmel High School for Boys was the only Catholic high school in all of Lake County, and it was run by the Carmelite order of priests and brothers. There was a mystique about Carmel: it drew kids from many towns around Mundelein, all the teachers were men, and we had to wear neckties, not the goofy little-kid ties that we'd worn at Santa Maria but real ones like businessmen wore to work. We SMdPers were more than ready to get down to business—to make our mark. I had an advantage over many of my friends because I had two brothers who had recently graduated from Carmel. The gang would have to come to me for the inside scoop.

I entered Carmel in the fall of 1973 as the school was beginning to experiment with a modular scheduling system, which gave the students an "open campus" and a discernable sense of freedom. Since Carmel was a college-prep school, the theory was that this system would better prepare us for the independence of college. When we had free periods with no classes scheduled, we were not assigned to be anywhere in particular, such as in a designated study hall as at most other high schools. The intention was

for us to use our free time on our own—like college students—
to prepare for upcoming classes, study for tests, and complete
assignments. Instead, when we didn't have classes, most of us were
like convicts on furlough. We found endless mischief to engage in
both on campus and off.

CARMELITES AND COEDS

Though we had no girls in our Carmel classrooms, girls were definitely on the scene, hundreds of them. Carmel High School for
Girls was the other half of our campus, connected by common
areas: a shared student lounge and cafeteria, library, chapel, theater, and gym. This was a boys' school, but not a school without
girls—the best of both worlds. We didn't worry about embarrassing ourselves if we were clumsy in the classroom, nor were we
tempted to show off by being oafish and macho. We reserved the
machismo for the lounge, where all the action was.

Our lounge was much like a singles bar for us hormonally
charged adolescents, filled with candidates of the opposite sex to
ogle and flirt with. Before entering, most kids—boys as well as
girls—would make a stop in the bathroom on their side of the
common area to primp for the "meet market." There was never
any residual shame from a dressing-down by a teacher, no feeling
foolish for boneheaded classroom behavior, no sense of academic
inadequacy. If a girl was superior in the classroom, she remained
a viable target of male attention in the lounge; attending separate
classes was a great equalizer. We boys told exaggerated stories of
how tough the priests were on us. The girls complained about the
close watch the nuns kept on their brood.

High school for me was a welcome change. With kids from
all over Lake County attending, I expanded my circle beyond the

Mundelein cohort and made many new friends. Though we were at an age when cliques define the social world and the drive to belong is typically strong, the class of '77 was special in that everyone seemed to be accepted by the group at large. No rigid social contract stratified us as jocks, geeks, or freaks; the labels were there, of course, but we didn't feel uncomfortable crossing the line from one group to another. I was as comfortable hanging out with athletes as I was with the dope-smokers or the bookworms.

When I wasn't in class my freshman year, you'd be less likely to find me in the library than at the 7-Eleven a few blocks away. By the time I was a junior, I was probably out cruising in someone's car, and by senior year, it could have been a run to El Barrio Grocery or The Big Horn for brewskis. Just before the start of my junior year I bought a 1963 Cadillac Fleetwood, with the famous fins in the back, for $175. It was truly a junk, but I had more fun driving and taking care of that jalopy than the rich kids in their new cars would ever know. I rigged a cheap but obnoxiously loud eight-track stereo system with nine speakers hanging from various parts of the interior. Friends loved to go on double dates with me (for obvious reasons), and when it was boys' night out, I always drove, because we could easily fit seven or eight of us—or if the drive-in was our destination, a few more in the trunk.

The car had started out deep blue, but the original paint had oxidized, giving the finish an iridescence that literally changed colors depending on how the light hit it. I once escaped big trouble with Father Tony, the diminutive young priest who was in charge of discipline for our class, because some other kid snitched that he saw a "purple tank" smash another car in the school parking lot. When I denied any knowledge of the incident, Father Tony winked at me and told the snitch, "It couldn't be O'Donnell—his car is blue." The guy I bought the car from had stenciled *Bitter*

Blue across the hood to add to the hippie mystique of the ride, and it backed my story that day.

HARD ACTS TO FOLLOW

I was the third O'Donnell boy to enter Carmel, and I didn't know what a legacy was until then. My eldest brother, Bob, was a straight-A student and a model Carmel citizen: he was quiet and well behaved, never got into any trouble, and was very much involved in the school community. He didn't make headlines, but he made an impression on every teacher on campus. His preparation for classes and tests was legendary (and bordered on the obsessive). He had a small circle of friends and a sweetheart he would later marry. Bob was five years ahead of me in school and he set the academic bar ridiculously high.

My second brother, Tom, four years ahead of me, had graduated the year before I entered Carmel. Tom was also a good student, but more importantly the star athlete of his class. Tom *did* make headlines for his gridiron exploits, and I was his biggest fan. In grade school I kept a scrapbook of the many pictures and stories about him in the local press. Unlike Bob, Tom had a large circle of friends and cut a wide social swath. He never got into big trouble, but he was a lively and very popular teenager; he dated many Carmel girls and even cast his net out to other schools as his good looks, confidence, and charm opened doors. There was talk of him playing big-time college football (Notre Dame, of course) until a devastating knee injury ended that dream—another bar set ridiculously high for the third O'Donnell to come along.

When I arrived at Carmel, I was ill prepared for the high expectations of me. Teachers expected me to be as diligent and studious as Bob and seemed disappointed to find I was not. Coaches, especially football coaches, expected me to be as vigorous and talented as Tom and at first refused to believe I wasn't going to blossom into him either. But I was decidedly neither one of my brothers—or maybe I was a diluted version of both. I was not as aggressive as Tom on the football field nor as dedicated and disciplined in the classroom as Bob. I was average in most ways. I was an unremarkable athlete and a marginal student lacking interest in most academic subjects, with one notable exception: religion.

It's not that I was a holy-roller type of kid. I was actually kind of a smart-ass. But I was interested in the topic of religion, and the priests taught it very differently than the nuns had. Religion class at Carmel was much more interesting and expansive than in grade school, less focused on catechism and not very much into rote. The curriculum delved into morality, ethics, and social issues. We discussed abortion, the death penalty, poverty, and civic responsibility. We debated birth control, sex, and marriage. There was more political and social awareness being cultivated than there was doctrine or dogma being hawked. The focus seemed to be more on molding us into good men than on training us to give the "right" answers.

I enjoyed the real-world feeling of these classes. We read books, watched films, and had open discussions about them, and the priests seemed interested in our opinions. The questioning and quarrelling that had made me the bane of the nuns' existence turned into debate that the priests actually encouraged. They even tolerated my sometimes rebellious attitude. Since we stayed away from catechism almost entirely, I didn't run into the mystery-of-faith dilemma I'd continually encountered with the nuns; the issues we discussed called for more dialogue and less top-down instruction, and I liked this kind of engagement much better than backing a teacher into a corner over the logic of the Virgin Birth. One year I got an A without attending a single class; instead I volunteered at a state developmental center and worked in group homes with mental patients. High school was the first time I'd ever been encouraged to think outside the box, applauded for challenging conventional wisdom, accepted for being contrarian, or rewarded for "doing" something instead of "learning" something. Having no girls in the classroom to either fear or show off for was a benefit, and having no nuns trying to push me back into the box was downright liberating. I began to expand ever so subtly in spiritual ways.

I even thought I sensed a vocation to the priesthood for a time. My interest in religion class, joined with a remote yet discernable desire to help other people, sounded like the faint beginnings of a calling. This was short-lived, though, and discouraged by the priests, of all people. When one of my best friends and I were thinking of living in The Carmel House—a home for future Carmelites—and went to discuss it with Father Ray, the priest who ran the house, he was initially very pleased to consider us. But Father Ray was new that year, and our overture was *not* taken seriously by the other priests, who had known us for a couple of years already. They could see we weren't viable candidates, mostly because they noticed we were very interested in girls. Father Ray was overruled and we were accused of making a mockery of the program. So much for my vocation; it lasted less than two weeks.

HOOP DREAMS

In the summer before seventh grade, I had begun attending a basketball camp in the beautiful and pristine Northwoods of Wisconsin run by a wonderful coach from Chicago, Ray Meyer, and his family. By high school I had a summer job there, working in exchange for my enrollment. The seemingly endless days were some of the best times of my life: 10 to 12 hours a day on a basketball court, doing the thing I loved most in life at the time and learning lessons that would serve me well much later. I learned leadership skills by having responsibility for other boys at the camp—many of them my own age or older, as the "campers" ranged from grade-school to college-age. I learned the value of hard work as I improved my skills by practicing and challenging myself against better players. I learned about discipline, and I learned by watching a truly amazing family in action, full of love and respect for one another and dedication to their work. Summers in Three Lakes, Wisconsin, were perfect: lots of sun, daily swimming in the chilly waters just downhill from camp, long runs through the hilly terrain, waterskiing, canoeing, silly pranks, and basketball—lots and lots of basketball. We had drills in the morning, games after lunch for the younger kids, and games after dinner for the high-school and college players, which were extremely competitive and hard-fought. It felt like a major promotion when I began to be selected to play in the evening games.

Ray Meyer, the head basketball coach at DePaul University for several decades, had built the rustic camp with his own hands. For a time, I felt a part of this great family, because they treated their staff like sons in both the caretaking and the discipline departments. "Coach," as everyone called him—even his wife, Marge, and his three sons—had a huge impact on the man I became. He was always teaching, always challenging, constantly prodding me to become a little better, to work a little harder, to do a little more than I thought I could. On Sunday mornings, when the drill schedule was lighter and the temptation to sleep in was strong, Coach would come into my cabin and literally pull me out of my bunk by my hair (long, blond, and curly in the style of the times) and insist that I attend Mass. He didn't make everyone go, just those of us who spent the whole summer with him and who were

Catholic. I fit both categories, so there was no escaping Mass for me. Even though I complained, I secretly appreciated the extra attention Coach paid to my religion and me.

The summer before my sophomore year, when my parents paid a visit to me at camp, we were all shocked to hear Coach say that although I wasn't good enough to play for him at DePaul, I should have every expectation of playing in college and getting at least a partial scholarship to some smaller school. He said he saw vast improvements in my game, and he insisted that my hard work would not go unrewarded. The confidence this gave me was amazing. I started playing at a level I never imagined I could. But though the confidence Coach had in me and the work ethic he instilled in me would benefit me in the long term, in the short term it did nothing to influence my high-school basketball career. Coach Krajacek back at Carmel didn't think I was such hot stuff. It turned out the biggest lesson I would get from high-school basketball was how to deal with devastating disappointment.

Coach Krajacek, who also taught math, was a fine basketball coach who had his own ideas and philosophy of the game; it just happened to be a very different philosophy than the one I had been taught all those years at camp. I remained true to what Coach Meyer had drilled into me and wrote Krajacek off as an amateur. The problem was that I didn't hide that opinion too well.

At camp, I was accustomed to being the one who set the tempo of the game. I was a decent ball handler, but, more importantly, well schooled in the key position of point guard; I knew how to run a team. I'd been mentored by the best coaches and tested against the best players. I went toe-to-toe with some of the best high-school players in the Chicago area and could hold my own against college players too. I didn't have the physical gifts of many of the elite players I played with at camp, but I was smart and tenacious; Coach

Meyer said I had a high basketball IQ. I understood the game better than some of those super-talented players. I was sure to have a noteworthy high-school career, play some ball at a small college, then become a coach, just like Coach Meyer and his sons.

Confidence in my game was one thing, but my unwillingness to adapt to the approach of my high-school coach was arrogant and disrespectful. At the time, though, I didn't realize how it got in the way of my goals on the court. I continued to practice the way I played at camp—to run the team the way *I* wanted and not the way my coach insisted. I wouldn't conform. Coach Ray Meyer himself had installed and approved my game, and no math teacher from the suburbs was going to take "my game" away from me. But he did just that, and in the most literal way. On Friday and Saturday nights, when I believed I should be leading the Carmel basketball team on the court, I was seated next to Coach Krajacek on the bench.

In the winter of my senior year, disheartened and finally fed up, I walked into the coach's office to ask him if I could practice with the team during the week but not suit up for games on the weekends. "I just can't take sitting on the bench anymore," I explained. The bitterness of watching other players get the minutes and the glory that were supposed to be mine was too much for me. "I still love the game, and I'll show up for every practice," I promised Coach. "I'll work hard and challenge your starters during the week to get them ready for games."

Coach didn't even have to think it over. "Absolutely not," he said. He asked me to stick it out, and I agreed. But as I walked away from his office through the cool, dark gym, I sensed that nothing would change. I went back into the office and told him I was sticking to my original decision. "Coach, I'm leaving the team."

"I'm sorry to hear that, Tim, but it's your decision," was all he said.

Why did I flip-flop so quickly? I went from quitting to staying to quitting again, all in the span of five minutes or so. I was conflicted about leaving the team, but totally disgusted at sitting on the bench. I sure could have used a good talk with Coach Meyer at that point, but I was just beginning to learn to make my own way. I was responding to an intuition that was new and scary, but also powerful and kind of exhilarating—at least in that moment.

The decision to quit basketball was one of the few choices I would ever regret in my life, and its effect on me was immediate and profound. I lost focus and began to drift. It was hard to concentrate on school, I felt distanced from my friends on the team, I withdrew from my family, and with nothing positive to do after school, I became a little self-destructive, smoking more pot and dwelling on how I'd been "wronged." Without basketball, I felt angry, betrayed, and lost. I'd worked hard, I'd studied the game I loved, and now my dream of playing in college and becoming a coach like Coach Meyer was dying before my eyes. My heart was broken. And I was suffering silently: I didn't believe I had anyone to talk to about the way I was feeling, so I turned the bitterness inside.

FREEBIRD

During the last semester of my senior year, I got more and more restless. I was bitter about the way basketball had ended, and school felt pointless without it. For the first time, I began to question the purpose of my life. Did it even *have* a purpose? What would I do without basketball? How could I recover from such a loss? It was what I thought I lived for. To make things worse, I believed I had no one to turn to with these feelings. I had a sense of wonder bordering on fantasy about the way my life would go, yet I had no guidance to get there, and now the direction that basketball had given me was gone.

One cold and gloomy Tuesday afternoon, home alone, I went into my mom's room and took several hundred dollars from a drawer where I knew she always kept cash. I left a note telling her not to worry, that I was leaving and didn't know when I would return, but that I promised to pay her back. I explained I wasn't mad at anyone; I just needed to get away. I felt I would suffocate if I didn't leave that very moment. I didn't know what I was running to or from, but I was running nonetheless.

It was February 1977, the dead of winter. I packed some clothes and assembled an appropriate road-trip soundtrack of eight-track tapes—Lynyrd Skynyrd ("Freebird"), the Allman Brothers ("Ramblin' Man"), the Grateful Dead, ("Goin' Down the Road Feelin' Bad"), Boston ("Foreplay/Long Time"). Throw in a pipe for smoking pot and I was off. I was heading west to "find myself," in the catchphrase of the time. I thought I was going to end up in California, see the ocean for the first time, maybe become a star or something, I didn't know. I just heard a call to hit the road and I didn't hesitate or debate. It was the first time I heard and listened to this call from deep within my soul, but it would not be the last.

Once on the road, I was exhilarated like never before. I was totally at ease driving the interstate, stopping along the way when I needed to, on nobody's schedule but mine. This was before the big family-friendly travel centers and the interstate interchanges clogged with fast-food restaurants and chain motels. Off the interstate in those days you found only the basics: gas stations that mainly just sold gas, with cigarette machines and the occasional vending machine that dispensed candy bars, pop, and chips. I bought junk food at the truck stops and slept in my car at the rest areas along the highway. I found lots of other people sleeping in cars and vans there, and I felt like I was part of some subculture of the road—lots of hippies with rock music and the smell of pot smoke filling the air. Strangely, I felt I belonged.

After a couple of days of driving, I remembered that a friend from Carmel, a kid named Henry, had moved to Arlington, Texas, the year before. From a pay phone outside of Texarkana, I called him very late one night and told him I was on the road to California and I was going to stop in and see him. Boy, did that sound cool. I drove through the night, catching some sleep along the way, and got to his house about 6:30 the next morning. We concocted a story for his parents that I was visiting colleges in the area and wouldn't be staying more than a couple of days. His dad was wise to my story, but pretended to believe us; his mom appeared oblivious to my presence.

Henry went to school that morning and I slept until he got home. That night it snowed a couple of inches, and school was called off the next day, a Friday. That much snow in Chicago barely registered, but it was an event in Texas. We cruised around suburban Dallas in Henry's VW bus the entire weekend, meeting girls from his new school and impressing them with the story of this "ramblin' man" from Chicago making his way to California. The affluent suburbs of Dallas seemed another world from the one I'd left. The homes were big and fancy, the moms were all pretty, and the kids all had nice clothes and new shoes. Henry's house was bigger than his old one and he had a huge recreation room above the garage all to himself where I slept during my stay.

Henry himself had changed in some ways, and I grudgingly admitted to myself that the change was good for him. I got the impression that his dad had taken this transfer to Dallas mostly to get Henry away from the influence of his friends back home, the boys from Carmel (like me) who were running wild on the "open campus" we all abused. Like most of the rest of our class, Henry had been a pothead at Carmel, but he was on his way to becoming a model citizen in Arlington. I began to notice his dad looking at me with growing suspicion; he figured out I had reintroduced Henry to smoking pot and he wasn't very happy about it.

After a couple of days, Henry's dad had had enough of my charade. Over grits and eggs one morning, he asked, "What schools here in Texas are you looking into?" My masquerade as the college-bound student shopping for schools crumbled with one question. I didn't even have a clue what schools were in the area!

"I know you two have been smoking marijuana," Henry's dad went on, and proceeded to lecture us about the evils of the weed. He was a scientist of some sort, and he was emphatic in explaining that research had "proven without a doubt that smoking leads you to use hard drugs." But the conversation was somewhat one-sided, because Henry and I were stoned. Usually glib, I had nothing to say for myself. Then Henry's dad insisted I call home. The game was over. It was actually a relief to quit pretending.

When I told my mother I was safe, she was too relieved to be angry—or even to let me finish talking. "I'm in Arlington—"

"Oh, thank God," she shrieked, "you're in Arlington Heights!" That was a suburb of Chicago about 20 minutes from home. When I interrupted her jubilation with the news that I was in fact in Arlington, *Texas,* she began to panic. "I'm sending you a plane ticket home," she insisted. "Your old junk of a car is in no condition to make the trip." I knew she was right, there was a risk that the car wouldn't make it, but I was even more insistent that I get myself back home to Mundelein: "I got myself into this, and I want to get myself out of it." Since she had no way of forcing me, she had to give in.

Suddenly, I wanted desperately to go home. I wanted to finish school and I wanted to go to college. I was sure I was in trouble at Carmel; everyone was looking for me, and the priests wouldn't react kindly to an unauthorized winter break. I had missed the better part of two weeks and I knew the risk of getting kicked out of Carmel was very real.

If Henry's dad hadn't seen through my act, I might have continued to believe my own "story" and kept on traveling west with only the meager resources I had left. As I climbed into the car, Henry gave me a cool parting gift: a tape by a band called Head East. More excellent traveling music, and a sort of stoner's compass as I retraced my route along the interstate. I never did thank either of them properly for getting me headed back in the right direction.

During this little adventure, I began to distinguish a sort of voice inside. I had noticed it before, but this was the first time it sounded like anything more than background noise. I was beginning to recognize, ever so faintly, a knowingness beyond explanation, beyond my own intelligence or knowledge. I would later learn to understand this as intuition, and later still something even grander than intuition, but at the time, I just listened. It felt and sounded separate from my own voice in some way. I welcomed the company of this voice that suspended my restlessness a little and offered a sense of peace and well-being that had been missing since I quit basketball.

HOMEWARD BOUND

On the trip home, I noticed people were very interested in my plight. Two or three gas-station attendants noticed the threads showing through the rubber tread of my tires. One guy even offered me a set of used tires free, explaining that my own had just a few miles before they gave out altogether. There was oil leaking, the heat quit working, and I was afraid to turn the engine off for fear that it would not start again. It rained, sleeted, or snowed the whole way back to Mundelein, but I never doubted my safe return.

In the silence and solitude of that cold trip home, I contemplated what little I knew about life. I began to wonder why the nuns taught us we should fear God, when I was beginning to feel a warm and loving presence within that I thought must be He. I began to question all the ritual I had grown up with. I knew I was closer to God in my dying old Caddy, hungry and cold on the interstate, than I ever had been in the comfort of a pew. I had been misled, and I was getting mad.

I had noticed several bumper stickers on my drive through the South that proclaimed, "Jesus Loves You." Really? Not according to the nuns. Jesus, God, or whoever was always mad at me, always looking for a reason to punish me, always ready to give me the "blessing" of suffering so I could emulate the suffering of Jesus on the Cross. None of it made sense any longer. I was going home, I was going to graduate, and then I was going to walk—no, *run* away from the Catholic Church.

When I got home, there were several of my friends keeping vigil with my mom, reassuring her I'd return safely. When I parked my car in the driveway and turned the ignition off, it gave a loud hissing noise and red fluid rushed out the bottom of the car like blood on the snow. Bitter Blue died on the spot that cold winter night and never started again. The next day we ceremoniously towed it to the junkyard and I got $75 from the scrap man. Even this coincidence—the car dying only after getting me home—took on a mystical quality in my view. The "voice" that told me I would get home was right. This voice I would come to trust as my life continued to unfold.

Back at Carmel, a debate raged among the priests as to what should be done with me. There was a contingent of teachers and administrators bent on expelling me from school. They felt they couldn't just let a kid take off for a couple of weeks and return without any consequences whatsoever. Luckily for me, there was also Father Tony.

I don't really know how, when, or why Father Tony became a champion of mine, but every time I found myself in trouble, he was there to keep it from getting out of hand. He took my side in almost every scrap and fracas I got into, and there were more than just a few. This time, I thought I might have pushed even him too far. But I explained to him anyway why I had done what I did. I didn't make any excuses or tell him any tales, I just told him I was confused and needed time alone. I explained that the abrupt disappearance of basketball from my life had probably affected me more than I cared to admit. And this wonderful little Irish priest from Canada ferociously defended me in the face of his brethren and the administration and kept them from kicking me out.

Without his intervention and strong advocacy, there's no telling how different the course of my life might have been. If I had been kicked out of Carmel, I probably would have quit school in the same way I quit basketball, bitter and brokenhearted. I think Father Tony suffered some consequences, not only for defending me but for the way he handled our class in general, as he was transferred away at the end of that school year—though not before he attended the senior prom with my date and me, so attached to him had I become. He would return years later to preside over my wedding as well.

The trip to Texas might have been the beginning of my sense that a higher power, one I had been trained to call God, was in the driver's seat of my life—or at least riding shotgun. I got away with it, all of it. The car that was barely roadworthy kept me safe for hundreds of miles in the dead of winter, the priests who wanted my head were held at bay, and I returned a hero to my mates.

Even my mom shrugged it off with a wry smile. I felt invincible, protected by an unseen force.

The last few months of high school were a whirl of parties, celebrations, and investigating substances of higher consciousness. With graduation and freedom in sight, alcohol and drugs began to play a bigger part in the life of our class than they ever had. We teenagers of the '70s thought we were pretty well-informed about the dangers of drugs; you see, the kids from the '60s were the guinea pigs, they experimented with *everything*, and by the time it was our turn to partake, we thought we already *knew* what would kill you. We were investigating drugs to enhance our experiences and some of us began to believe we just might be expanding our consciousness in the process. Were we actually able to "see God," as some of us claimed? That's very doubtful, but try telling that to a kid under the influence of '60s music (we loved their music) and hallucinogens. We were tempting fate by toying with danger, but in our last few months together we felt pretty bulletproof. As for me, I was just beginning the pattern of seeing things through a metaphysical monocle; to my way of thinking, even adolescent experimentation with dangerous drugs became a transcendent spiritual event.

BUILDING ON THE FOUNDATION

Leaving the clutches of Catholic education in grade school, I had been full of fear and foreboding about God and his judgment. Leaving high school, I was beginning to feel a spiritual companionship in my life. Could this presence be the same God I had been so afraid of just a few years before? For the moment, I wasn't focused on the doctrine of my religion that put God in a remote place "up there"; I was focusing on my own experience that was just beginning to make God feel approachable "down here."

As I moved on from high school to what we half-jokingly, half-anxiously called the real world, I was gaining optimism about a relationship with God, although still dubious about the Catholic Church. My personal beliefs were changing form:

- I had survived the disappointment of basketball. I was stronger than I thought I was.

- There was more to life than sports. There was more to *me* than sports. I was more than my physical self.

- There was something spiritual and unexplainable in my own life. Maybe Spirit was not remote, not "up there," but here and now.

- Perhaps we were less separated from God than the nuns had taught.

- The Catholic Church was too ritualistic. I was resentful and suspicious that the church was blocking my relationship with God because of the position it laid claim to in my life.

God was beginning to feel personal, like a real presence I could trust. I believed God had been on the trip to Texas with me. By contrast, the Catholic Church (except for Father Tony) was still an unfriendly, impersonal institution. It was beginning to seem as though the Church wanted me to have a relationship with the Church itself first and foremost, and that this got in the way of a possible relationship with God. Even so, I wasn't quite ready to abandon the Church. I decided I should educate myself about it first. Then I could leave with a clear conscience.

FOUR

WHAT IS RELIGION?

Putting God on Paper

As universal as the human desire to know God is, it might seem logical that the primal question would find an equally universal answer among the family of man. Not so—not even close.

Mankind's answer to its own Ascending Urge is formal religion, and religion is just about as charged and divisive a topic as you can think of. If you want to start an argument, get two or more people talking about religion and watch their respective positions harden into battle lines. This is why well-mannered people avoid the subject in social settings, business meetings, family gatherings, and other situations where protocol (or political correctness) dictates staying away from potentially inflammatory topics. Any difference in beliefs is hard for us humans to take, and religious differences stir up particularly deep feelings. Yet differences are inevitable: even two people from the same religious tradition seldom agree on all aspects of their belief system.

Most of the violence and bloodshed in our recorded history has risen out of these gaps between beliefs. In the last century alone, at least a hundred million people were killed in the name of religion—

as a conservative estimate. Much of the conflict in the world today is due to such differences as well. At the time of this writing, people are being killed in Afghanistan, Gaza, the Congo, Iraq, Nepal, Rwanda, Sri Lanka, and Sudan—just to name a few—because of differing beliefs. Zealots attack innocents on a daily basis in the name of one belief system or another, and then these zealots are labeled "terrorists" or "evildoers" and attacked in turn in the name of a different set of beliefs. Turn on the news and you'll probably hear about a crime committed in your own city because one person believes something different from another: churches are burned, epithets are scrawled on walls, people are beaten and killed, all because one disagrees with another's beliefs about one thing or another.

The desire to know Truth may be universal but the way we go about finding it is most certainly not. The progression in human understanding that gave shape to the world's many religious belief systems may have led them in the same general direction, toward monotheism, but the rituals and doctrines these systems produced vary widely. Religion comes from the human mind attempting to answer questions originating in the human spirit. And as is normally the case, it is nearly impossible to get the individual minds of humans to collectively draw one common conclusion.

When we start to ask how the same primal search led us to such different places, we confront a whole new set of questions.

Is religion the natural, inevitable response to mankind's Ascending Urge?

Was religion a divine gift to mankind, or did we invent it?

Was religion delivered by people called prophets?

Is one religion "truer" than another?

Is there such a thing as Absolute Truth?

Can religion in any way progress or evolve?

Is organized religion the only path to God?

History shows that we humans do not like our beliefs to be challenged, and religious beliefs seem to be the most brittle and volatile of them all. Some religions are so bent on being right (and everyone else being wrong) that they make it an explicit part of their mission to convert the world to their way of thinking. The word *religion* comes from a Latin root that means to tie or bind. So why does organized religion divide us instead of connecting us?

STRETCHING (FOR) THE TRUTH

Shortly after turning 40, I decided to stop taking my good health for granted. I learned more about what to eat and what to avoid, I revamped my exercise routine, and I looked for a stretching program to loosen my increasingly stiff joints. At my local Target, I found a CD called *AM & PM Yoga for Beginners* by a young man named Rodney Yee. I found his instruction on the basics of yoga easy to understand and I began to feel positive results right away.

Sounds innocent enough, right? Well, not exactly, as it turned out. When I investigated a little about yoga I was shocked to learn it was very much frowned upon by the Catholic Church. I don't wish to get off on the considerable tangent of the dangers yoga supposedly presents for Christendom, but I'll share a few of the most curious condemnations:

Since yoga focuses on the physical body, it directs one's mind away from God. Yoga encourages practitioners to clear their minds, and emptying your mind leaves it open to evil influences—namely Satan. Yoga finds its origin in Hinduism, which believes humans can merge with God, and since the Hindu god is not the same as the Christian one, the practice leads Christians away from the one true God. Yoga meditation attempts to turn off all thoughts; when Christians meditate, they should meditate on the word of God. Yoga encourages practitioners to focus on the self, which glorifies the creature, whereas all glory should go to the Creator. All of the yoga poses are imitations of animal postures and warped versions of worship. Every yoga posture was originally designed to worship a Hindu god. And so forth and so on.

Jeez! All I really wanted to do was to learn to stretch properly, and maybe fend off the effects of Father Time. The six or seven poses I added to my daily routine very quickly made me feel suppler and my joints stopped creaking. Yoga was never presented to me as a *religious practice* and I didn't make it into one. It was no more and no less *religious* than running on my treadmill or lifting weights. These so-called threats to my Christianity seemed altogether ridiculous and paranoid.

But they did capture my curiosity about *other* religions. What did critics in the Church mean when they used terms like "Hindu god"? Another God? I got very curious about other cultures' definition of God: was it different from my understanding? Was Buddha greater than Krishna? Was Jesus more holy than Moses? Was Muhammad really the last prophet? What exactly did the other belief systems have to say about Truth?

THE FACTS OF FAITH

Hundreds of groups in the world today call themselves "religions." Each one is saturated with colloquial and culturally specific language. Many are pegged to ancient levels of human comprehension and linked to archaic customs and mores. Most are rich in tradition, steeped in doctrine, and often intricate and beautiful. And nearly all lay claim to Universal Truth and absolute knowledge of God. Nevertheless, most were formulated when humans *believed* the world was flat, the sun revolved around the earth, and women were a form of deficient human being; before we *discovered* gravity, electricity, or the molecular nature of matter; and well before we *invented* the printing press, the telephone, or the automobile.

Throughout my considerable Catholic education I had learned very little about any other religions. I was always taught that Catholicism was the one true religion and that even other Christian denominations offered only a partial version of Truth. But as my education took me deeper into Catholic culture and doctrine, it never actually included any real information about other belief systems—where they came from, who practiced them, what they taught. My education about religion was deep but not very wide. It took me a long time to discover that when examining one's own beliefs, it's helpful to get some perspective by looking at others.

After my run-in with Rodney Yee, as my own quest for Truth went on, I decided to get some perspective by surveying the so-called great religions of the world. I knew I would find obvious differences, but to my surprise, I found the differences did not necessarily amount to contradictions. Instead, I sensed more in common than I ever thought possible.

My investigation into these *other* religious belief systems was informal and done without benefit or burden of professional instruction. I started with first principles: what is a religion, anyway? A religion is a particular framework of faith and worship, a belief system built around a superhuman entity known as a *deity* or a god—a "phenomenon of being" or a spirit believed to have power over nature and/or human destiny and typically (but not always) believed to be responsible for creation. The religion dedicated to the god develops a comprehensive methodology outlining tenets and truths, expectations of adherents, and procedures for interacting with the god—namely, how to worship and appease it. Most religions have an organized system of beliefs, rules, and practices, collectively known as *doctrine.*

Typically, a religious belief system is introduced by an individual who claims some connection to the Divine. This person is usually labeled a prophet and the divine message he delivers is called *revelation.* The revelation may be delivered to the prophet by a messenger from God, often an angel, such as the one who spoke to Muhammad; the deity may deliver the message directly, as God did to Moses; or the message may come via inspiration in some mystical or enlightened state of consciousness, as in the case of the Buddha. The revelation is then disclosed to followers and a *deposit of belief* is made into the human consciousness.

In many cases, the prophet's followers view him as a deity in his own right. Accordingly, the deposit of faith is believed to be *absolute* Truth, which renders all other prophets and their messages incomplete or false. Such exclusive claims to absolute Truth are the cause of the strongest intolerance for other religious belief systems. If you are taught to believe that the "depositor" of your particular belief system is a deity—and that there is only one deity—you'll naturally conclude that all others are impostors. The positions become rigid, the language gets strident, and suddenly differing belief systems are blasphemous or evil and their adherents heretics or infidels.

There are five religions today that account for about 75 percent of the world's population. The youngest of the five is fourteen hundred years old. Each one was formulated by the followers of the enlightened mystic who made the original deposit of faith or by the mystic himself. Each of these five has dozens of breakaway denominations or sects. Perhaps the most interesting characteristic they share is that they remain relatively unchanged since the time of their original deposits as much as three thousand years ago.

The following is not a comparative survey of great religions; I offer it here to provide a little of that perspective I just mentioned.

HINDUISM

One of the oldest surviving formalized religions we know of, though almost certainly not the first, is Hinduism. The word for the Supreme Being (god) in Hinduism is *Brahman*. The essence of Brahman is infinite being, infinite awareness, and infinite bliss; the form of Brahman may take many shapes, known as incarnations. These incarnations may be in human form or in the forms of icons. Human versions of Brahman are known as Avatars and they come to assist men in times of need.

Although there is a pantheon of Hindu gods and goddesses, each god or goddess is an individual and separate incarnation or expression of the singular and infinite Brahman. It is easy to label Hinduism polytheistic, and by some standards it may be, but from the perspective that Brahman, the Infinite Awareness, is incarnated through these other gods and goddesses, Brahman is the monolithic being or essence that gives Hinduism the character of a monotheistic faith.

There is no single person credited with starting Hinduism, and its origin is in such a remote past that it is difficult to date, but it is commonly thought to coincide with the birth of Krishna about 3228 BCE. (Some scholars believe Hinduism dates back to

10,000 BCE.) Hinduism is a tolerant and diverse religion open to wide interpretation.

Hinduism teaches there is life after death through reincarnation *(Samsara)*. It teaches that a person's chief responsibility is to live virtuously *(Dharma)*. It holds that a soul achieves liberation from Samsara *(Moksha)* through the law of right action *(Karma)*.

Hinduism is the oldest organized religion in existence today and the third largest in the world, with about one billion adherents, some 16 percent of the world's population. About 90 percent of Hindus live in India.

BUDDHISM

Buddhism claims no singular, supreme creator of the universe and no savior or judge of mankind. For these reasons, some people claim that Buddhism is not a religion at all, but a *spiritual philosophy*. Some even call it atheistic, but this depends on your definition of God. In Buddhism, the highest form of being is the *Awakened Self*, which is a state of bliss called *Nirvana*.

Buddhism originates with a wealthy prince, Siddhartha Gautama, who was born in 563 BCE in northern India. When the prince ventured from his sheltered environment, where even the fact of death had been kept from him, he was affected deeply by the human suffering he witnessed. At about the age of 30, after an unsuccessful foray into asceticism, the prince achieved spiritual awakening while meditating under a sacred fig tree, where he reached *Bodhi*, or enlightenment. Siddhartha was thereafter referred to as the Buddha. The Buddha rejected the idea that he was a god; he simply said he had awakened. *Buddha* means "Awakened One."

The Buddha became a teacher, but he didn't teach what he learned in the awakened state; he taught people how to *achieve* the awakened state through their own experience instead of through a belief in dogma. That said, there are teachings in Buddhism, organized into four truths, five precepts, and an eightfold path of practice. The Four Noble Truths of Buddhism acknowledge human suffering, identify attachment as the cause of it, and posit an end to suffering via a path away from attachment. One reaches spiritual enlightenment when one is able to drop attachment to desire and to self. Buddhists believe in life after death through reincarnation.

Buddhism eventually declined in India but spread to Asia and flourished there. Today it is the fourth largest religion in the world, with about 376 million adherents, or 6 percent of the world population. There are several sects of Buddhism, largely defined by geographic regions, but they generally share a core set of beliefs. One of the branches, Zen Buddhism, is gaining particular popularity in the West.

JUDAISM

Another ancient religion, Judaism, is very small in comparison to these other four and the forerunner to the two largest, Christianity and Islam. It identifies the singular Supreme Being as Yahweh, the god of a specific, chosen desert people, who made a covenant with them to effect their exodus from bondage to the Egyptians in exchange for adherence to His law.

From Yahweh the Jewish people received order and social justice, a clear understanding of right and wrong, and a code laid down for them to abide by. They arrived at these laws not by reason, but by *revelation:* God revealed the Law to Moses and Moses delivered it to his people via the Ten Commandments.

It isn't entirely clear if Jews were monotheists from the very beginning or gained this understanding over time. The Jewish monotheistic belief system as it took shape eliminated the pantheon of gods, and Yahweh was not part of nature but transcended it. Yahweh gave the Jewish people a singular object of their loyalty; there would be no allegiance to another god or to a king or emperor. "No other god before me" became a primary tenet of Judaism.

Although Jewish tradition traces its lineage back through creation to Adam, a man named Abraham, born in Mesopotamia in approximately 1800 BCE, is believed to have made a pact with Yahweh in Canaan that began the religion. Abraham was the first Jew to claim there was only one God, benevolent and omnipotent.

According to Judaism, the responsibility of a Jew is to live in compliance with the Law that was handed down from Yahweh directly to the Jewish people. The central text is the Torah, believed to have been authored by God and written by the hand of inspired prophets. Judaism is perhaps the first religion to identify a single and benevolent deity who acts out of love for His chosen people.

Today, there are about 13 to 14 million Jews in the world, with about 40 percent living in Israel. This accounts for less than one-half of one percent of the world's population. But though very small by percentage, Judaism has been a prominent player in world history and remains a geopolitical (and theopolitical) force in the world to this day.

CHRISTIANITY

Christianity teaches that God is a *triune* entity, that there are three persons within the one God. The Trinity is the Christian Church's central *mystery of faith,* the one mystery from which all other mysteries emanate (including the ones that puzzled me in grade school). To the non-Christian world, the concept of a triune God can be controversial, as it seems to break with the fundamental tenets of monotheism. Some other monotheistic belief systems of the world—especially the other *Abrahamic* religions, Islam and Judaism—impeach Christianity as something other than mono- theistic. (We'll discuss the Trinity in more detail in chapter 8.)

Christianity arose in the aftermath of the crucifixion of Jesus of Nazareth in 32 CE as his teachings were spread by a group of his followers known as *Apostles*. Jesus was a Jewish reformer who preached mainly in the towns, villages, and countryside of rural Palestine. Tradition holds that Jesus was born in Bethlehem; little is known of his life (except the famous story of his birth) until he began his ministry at around 30.

The teachings of Christianity are represented mainly in the Christian Bible, which combines the Jewish Torah with the 27 books of the New Testament. In addition to the Bible, the faith is expressed in many supplemental creeds and volumes of additional doctrine. Christianity declares that Jesus is the Messiah promised in Jewish scripture and that he is the only Son of God, born of a virgin. It claims that Jesus offered mankind a new covenant to replace the covenant between God and the Jewish people; this New Covenant is not exclusive to Jews but is available to all of man- kind. It teaches that Jesus rose from the dead three days after he was crucified, and his *resurrection* is the central tenet of the faith.

Christianity posits life after death, its quality determined by the type of life one has lived: a soul goes either to Heaven to be in the presence of God or to eternal punishment in Hell. It teaches, further, that a person's soul will be reunited with his body at the end of time on Judgment Day.

Christianity has fragmented over the centuries into three major sects: Roman Catholicism, Eastern Orthodoxy, and Protestantism. The Catholic Church claims *Apostolic Succession,* or an unbroken chain of leaders going back to Peter, one of Jesus'

Apostles, and thereby claims authority for teaching and interpreting the faith. Many Protestant denominations broke from the Catholic Church, headquartered in Rome, over political and doctrinal issues. The Eastern Orthodox Church, which also claims Apostolic Succession, is more closely tied to Rome but has its own headquarters and hierarchy.

Christianity is the largest belief system in the world, with over two billion adherents or approximately 33 percent of the world's population. It is the dominant belief system in Europe and the Americas.

ISLAM

The name of God in Islam is *Allah,* and the faith is emphatically monotheistic. Islam did not introduce monotheism to the world; it acknowledges Abraham as the father of monotheism. The major Islamic contribution to monotheism is the elimination of religious idols altogether. Islam offers no image of Allah, as God is unseen and invisible. There are no icons, no statues, no visual imagery in religious practice at all.

The most important (and perhaps misunderstood) aspect of Allah is his absolute power. The omnipotence of Allah is the most dominant characteristic and his power inspires fear. A fear of such omnipotence is appropriate and necessary. Allah is all-powerful and in control of the entire universe. There are consequences for not obeying Allah. *Islam* means *submission to God;* a practitioner of Islam is called a *Muslim,* or *one who submits to God.*

Islam was founded by an Arab military and political figure who became known as the Prophet *Muhammad.* Muhammad was born in 570 CE and began to receive revelations from Allah through the angel Gabriel in about 610 CE. Muslims consider him the last prophet sent by God, sent to restore the original deposits of faith made by earlier prophets, including Adam, Abraham, Moses, and Jesus. Muslims believe that these prophets preached Islam as well, but that Jews and Christians alike have distorted the meaning of the teachings. The text of Islam is called the Qur'an, and it offers not only religious doctrine but instruction on most parts of life, ranging from diet to warfare to social matters.

There are approximately 1.5 billion Muslims in the world, or 21 percent of the population. Islam is the second largest religion in the world and the fastest-growing, expected to surpass Christianity between 2025 and 2050 CE. About 20 percent of all Muslims live in Arab countries; Indochina has the largest Muslim population in the world at approximately 150 million. Islam is the dominant religion in the Middle East, northern Africa, and parts of Asia.

FAITHS OF OUR FATHERS

These five belief systems account for about 75 percent of the world's population, as I've noted, with another billion, or 16 percent, claiming to be nonreligious, atheist, secular humanist, or agnostic. So these five major religions account for the overwhelming majority of people who *practice* religion.

And they all share a major problem: they are *ancient.*

Each of these belief systems is based on an original deposit of faith made in antiquity, and each has become *doctrinized* to such an extent that it cannot develop any further, even though our capacity to comprehend can and does. Mankind's capacity to comprehend has multiplied many times over since these original deposits were made, yet believers today are expected to adhere to the language and understanding of antiquity and communicate spiritual matters within a framework of belief systems deposited thousands of years ago without any allowance for man's intellectual evolution.

Jesus was pointing us to the Truth when he directed us inside. I believe Buddha was a pointer to the Truth as well, and he pointed in a similar direction. Abraham steered mankind in the right direction by pointing us toward monotheism. Muhammad was right to reveal that God is pure Spirit and invisible. The point is that the prophets of yesterday (and today) are all pointers to the one Universal Truth they were given a glimpse of and described in their own dialect. They all made deposits to human awareness in the language of their day and none of the languages are perfect. In every case, the deposits of faith made by the founders, or original pointers, of the main belief systems of this world have more in common than not. These various responses to the universal Ascending Urge initially formed around aspects of a common Truth. How did the paths diverge, and what happened to Truth along the way? It's worth taking a look farther back to see.

The earliest manifestation of piety, and the likely precursor to formalized, doctrinal religion, was a form of animism: man worshipped things in the physical world that surrounded him, believing spirits inhabited objects in nature, at first mostly plants and animals. Before writing was invented, these beliefs were passed along from generation to generation by oral tradition. As they were forwarded from one generation and one clan to another, rituals were naturally refined and revised. *Spiritual evolution* was occurring naturally as man repeatedly redefined his relationships with the physical world in which he resided and the metaphysical world he yearned to commune with. Beliefs and practices evolved and expanded as they were passed along.

Expanding from the worship of animals, some groups of humans probably began worshipping elements in nature, like wind, sun, fire, and rain; adoration shifted from the animal forms mankind knew and understood to the forces of nature beyond understanding or control. Was this where the first schism, or break in religious tradition, took place? We may never know, but it's intriguing to wonder. Did humans begin to kill one another because one group worshipped the sun and another a lion?

As mankind increased its capacity to understand—as we *evolved*—we increasingly organized our thinking about life, both physical and metaphysical. As humans began to inhabit the corners of the earth, the urge to commune with forces greater than themselves followed, and belief systems were modified in response to the changing scenery. Some civilizations would eventually *anthropomorphize,* or attribute human characteristics to, the forces in nature and develop a *pantheon* of gods that were believed to have dominion over the natural world. Greek mythology is a perfect example of this evolution in conceptual depictions of deities: from worshipping the sky, for example, man anthropomorphized "sky" into the god Zeus, "sun" into the god Helios, and so on. These gods were responsible for most phenomena in nature and most aspects of mankind's experience on earth, including the course of human history. Eventually, the polytheistic paradigms represented in the various pantheons evolved further to the logical monotheistic conclusion of a single supreme deity.

At some point in the evolution of human spirituality, special people began to appear with higher levels of consciousness, advancing ideas of spiritual truth. These spiritual pioneers, called prophets or seers, were considered sacred. The original deposits of faith they made into human consciousness laid the groundwork for the development of the world's great systems of belief— and these deposits were made in the vernacular of the culture and the time they lived in. Since human language is an idiosyncratic, man-made tool, the prophets didn't speak a universal language of

Truth; they spoke *contemporaneously* about timeless Truth in the parlance of their time.

REVELATION OR INNOVATION?

The nature of the human Ascending Urge is to worship what we cannot explain. So mankind's metaphysical awareness evolves as our ability to *explain* expands. Our insatiable desire to accumulate knowledge, coupled with our inborn spiritual yearning, has created a sort of moving target when it comes to the metaphysical. Each time we come to an expanded understanding of the physical world, the metaphysical target shifts just beyond our understanding. This continuous shifting kept humanity on a path to ever-expanding metaphysical awareness.

Until we started to write it down.

When mankind invented writing, something happened to the Truth the prophets spoke of. No longer handed down in constantly evolving oral tradition, Truth began to be formalized, preserved, and protected, passed on *unchanged* to subsequent generations.

There's no question that writing has been instrumental in documenting the ever-expanding accumulation of human knowledge, and it has preserved the loftier ideas of consciousness contained in the prophets' initial deposits—but it may also have helped to hinder the evolution of the spiritual awareness those deposits pointed toward. Once an articulation of "truth" was tacked to papyrus, it became law. Institutions, whole *religions,* began to form around these written "laws" and quickly developed resistance to change of any kind.

What's more, all of these belief systems depended upon *human language* to express their individual interpretation of Truth. And to speak of God, Allah, Brahman, or Yahweh—or Universal Truth by any name—in human language is difficult if not impossible. The paradox of trying to understand "God" is that the human mind is the wrong tool for the job. It's like trying to use a hammer to shape a piece of glass. The human mind is suited to comprehend the natural, physical world, but God is an infinite supernatural presence that exists in the metaphysical world, beyond natural laws. The only way a human mind can really conceive of the Infinite Being that is God is by the process of elimination. "The only literally accurate description of the Unsearchable of which the ordinary mind is capable," writes Huston Smith in his classic *The World's Religions,* "is *neti . . . neti,* not this . . . not this. If you traverse the length and breadth of the universe saying of everything you can see and conceive, 'not this . . . not this,' what remains will be God."[1]

Is it possible that our own words, and especially the written word, have held us back from knowing God? Does doctrine keep us boxed in, preventing us from evolving spiritually even as our minds continually expand their capacity for awareness? The question is worth considering. Before writing, mankind's beliefs continuously advanced toward a fuller understanding of metaphysics. Since the written word, most belief systems remain codified in the vernacular of antiquity almost exactly as they were originally deposited. The prophets communicated to their followers in the language of the culture they lived in. Would Jesus speak differently today about Truth than he did two thousand years ago? What about Moses? Buddha? Muhammad? Is it unreasonable to expect that man might understand his relationship to God today better than he did two or three millennia in the past?

The underlying Intelligence of the universe is evident from the preponderance of order within it, and the essence of this Infinite

Intelligence is what we as a species long to know. Ever since we arrived on earth via the evolution of matter, we've been seeking to connect with this Intelligence through many disciplines, always with our Ascending Urge as the driving force. We've stalked knowledge by way of philosophy, science, and theology in an attempt to ascertain the source, the purpose, and the destination of life. The Ascending Urge has propelled us forward through history seeking Truth as we go.

Science continually advances our understanding of the natural, physical world. Science never ceases asking questions—even questioning its own previous answers. The body of scientific knowledge continues to evolve even when in doing so it renders an earlier doctrine obsolete. Science is never satisfied that what we know now is the last word.

Religion, on the other hand, resists inquiry and rejects any evolution of understanding. It remains fastened to the ideas introduced by the enlightened mystics of antiquity, claiming that the answers to our primal questions lie in that wisdom exactly as deposited, with no need or possibility for enlargement, even as the species asking the questions evolves in its capacity to understand.

Throughout the history of our quest for knowledge, science and religion have coexisted in an uneasy pattern of mutual mistrust. As we go forward in the drama of history, we may discover that the separation has never been necessary. Isn't it likely that a prophet today would include the knowledge we now possess about the natural world whenever he or she spoke about Universal Truth, or God? Perhaps we will see the barriers fall and science and philosophy converge into what we might call a *theology of reality*.

Is this "theology" the *real* answer to our shared primal quest? Will it lead us to the ultimate goal of the Ascending Urge we have followed from the first? Is it possible that the path of each of the various culturally conditioned dialects of Truth leads to the same ultimate, universal comprehension of it?

After all, there are many mountain paths that lead to the same summit.

FIVE

DISILLUSION AND DISCOVERY

The University of Life

After my impromptu trip to Texas at the beginning of 1977, I began to think a lot about religion and spirituality, not that I made a clear distinction between them at the time. I had begun to feel, very subtly, a living spiritual presence on that trip with me. I was having more and more misgivings about the rituals of Catholicism, but at the same time I was becoming more certain about the reality of God. I didn't yet know a thing about any other religions, so I had nothing to compare Catholicism to. But my growing uncertainty about the Church, though visceral and vague, was very palpable. I was thinking about leaving the Church to seek a belief system that had less to do with ritual and offered a more direct approach to the Creator.

But I felt fearful and, of course, guilty—and the guilt of a Catholic can run very deep. The nuns of Santa Maria had implanted in me a tangible dread of questioning doctrine. I had been told for so long that the Roman Catholic Church held the exclusive claim to Truth that to simply reject it outright was unthinkable. It still spoke to me on an important level; the bumper stickers

I'd seen on the road—*Jesus Loves You*—struck a chord, even as they triggered my cynical "Oh, really?" reaction. I found Jesus, the person, an increasingly compelling and attractive figure, so I felt Christianity was a certainty for me. And if Jesus had really started this church, then I would sever my link to him if I rejected it.

The belief that Jesus formed the Catholic Church and appointed the Apostle Peter as its first leader creates a chain of authority that leads from Jesus directly to the present Pope. This doctrine, known as Apostolic Succession, had been one of the main tenets of our religious education from the earliest years at SMdP, and I found it pretty persuasive. I began to rationalize that I shouldn't hold Jesus accountable for the state of the institution today. It wasn't his fault that the men guiding it over the centuries had mismanaged it. If Jesus came to start a church, I reasoned, who was I to just walk away from it?

I needed to find the Truth for myself. I decided I would study theology, and at the end of my education, I would be able to make a more literate and informed decision. I wasn't going to let the influence of the nuns (on whom I now placed all the blame) push me away from the Truth. And I assumed the Truth would be found within the Church; once I learned more about it, that would both satiate my desire to know and lead me to a deeper understanding of God.

As I contemplated this course of action, I felt satisfied with myself. I wasn't going to turn my back on something that had been thriving for two thousand years just because I was ticked off at some nuns. That would have been an emotional and imma-ture approach to a very important decision in my life, and I, of course, was a paragon of maturity. (Yeah, right!) My plan to find the Truth I was seeking felt like the grown-up way to proceed.

MEET THE JESUITS

In an effort to satisfy the logical questions my left brain persistently asked, I made a rather unimaginative choice about where to start. I decided to follow my eldest brother's lead and apply to Marquette University in Milwaukee, Wisconsin. Marquette is run by Jesuits, an important (and historically controversial) order of priests dedicated to Catholic education and scholarship. There, I figured, I should be able to learn pretty much all I needed to know about the Church.

I was a typical college student of the late '70s, drinking my share of beer and smoking more than my share of grass. Most of my friends at Marquette were pragmatic in their educational pursuits, majoring in business, engineering, journalism, or one of the sciences. My dual interests of political science and theology were somewhat out of step with theirs, but given that Marquette was a Catholic university, it was not completely outlandish. Anyway, I didn't have a path laid out for my future as some of my friends did; college for me was about seeking answers to big, audacious questions in an attempt to reconcile the nuns' indoctrination with my budding sense of an interactive and internal spiritual life.

I spent the first few semesters at Marquette fulfilling basic liberal-arts requirements. I took history, Spanish, sociology, psychology, math, and so forth, mostly taught by rock-star professors to groups of students numbering in the hundreds. The first-level theology courses were required for all students, so these classes were basic and mundane.

After a couple of unremarkable years in college, I decided to step it up a little bit. I was looking for better and deeper answers to my questions about religion, and I was getting bored in Milwaukee. That road trip to Texas had left me with a yearning for adventure.

I was feeling the call from deep within to hit the road again, only this time I would devise a much more elaborate scheme than just hopping in a car and taking off. I was going to make a pilgrimage of this quest for answers. I was going Continental.

During the fall semester of my second year at Marquette, I began to explore study-abroad programs and found the university had a program in Spain. I had taken four years of Spanish at Carmel and two semesters already at Marquette, so it seemed logical to apply for it. Then I discovered another program that another Jesuit school, Loyola University of Chicago, had in Rome. I looked at a map of Europe and realized that Rome, being more centrally located, would make a better base for travel. And what better place to finally get to the bottom of those Catholic mysteries of faith than Rome? If I couldn't find the answers I was seeking at the very seat of Christianity, in the Eternal City, I reasoned, either the questions were unanswerable or I was asking the wrong ones.

A FORK (LIFT) IN THE ROAD

To save money for my year abroad, I decided to take the spring semester off and get a full-time job. I got work driving a forklift in a plastic factory across the street from the apartment I was sharing with Jimmy, my best friend since high school. Jimmy was the middle child in a family of eleven and the single most congenial person I have ever known. He was a hard-working kid from a distinctly blue-collar Catholic family. He had a job in a different factory, and we encouraged each other as we took our first steps into the working world.

I worked as a material handler for the plastic manufacturing company, which meant I moved large rolls and bins of plastic from machine to machine with a forklift. First, I would move large containers of plastic resin from the receiving area in the back to large extruding machines located throughout the plant, which would melt the resin and roll it up into huge rolls of various widths. These rolls weighed hundreds of pounds each and could not be handled without machinery. I would either place the rolls in bins for use at a later date or deliver them directly to the next machine in line, which would form the rolled plastic into sterile containers, then on to a printer, who would print a label on the plastic film, and finally on to the shipping department. Most of the product being made was for packaging medical equipment and supplies.

At first, I enjoyed the responsibility of keeping all the material in the entire plant organized and flowing. It was the first time since basketball camp I'd been in charge of anything. It felt kind of big and important, it felt good to have responsibility, and it was rewarding to serve an important function in a large, intricate workplace. Every morning at six, I found the material waiting for me to be reorganized in a systematic fashion. I enjoyed creating order from chaos, even if it was only organizing rolls of plastic.

Chaos is hardly an exaggeration. Each morning I would hop on my forklift to find that the material I'd left organized only 12 hours before was in a total shambles. At first it didn't bother me—it proved that my work was important and the plant wouldn't stay in order without me. But somehow the work became less satisfying when I learned that after my 12-hour shift ended, another material handler worked the opposite 12-hour shift from 6 p.m. to 6 a.m. This other material handler didn't seem to enjoy keeping things tidy the way I did, and night after night he let the material fall into disarray. I became resentful and even a little possessive of "my" material when I returned day after day to find bins and rolls strewn haphazardly all over the plant. A seed was being planted within me, though, despite the annoyance. The joy of bringing order to a workplace in tumult would someday become my calling, although it would have more to do with people than it would with plastic.

The people who worked at this factory were very different from the kids I hung around with at Marquette. Some were union employees, some were not, and soon I could easily distinguish between the two. The union employees were higher-paid, they were completely open in their criticism of the company and its managers, and they were condescending toward those of us who were not in the union. They had a special disdain for newbies like me who "worked too hard." Jimmy had it even worse at his factory. He was actually threatened in the parking lot by union members because he worked too hard. They told him directly that they weren't going to let him "raise the rate." This meant he was putting out more production flow than the union rate called for and management might use his production to attempt to raise the amount they all would be required to produce. This attitude flew in the face of the way we were both raised, but I was fascinated with trying to figure out these people: discovering what made them tick, what motivated them, and what concerned them became a private game for me.

At the same time, while following my curiosity, I began to meld with the culture of the factory. I went out to the local watering holes; I went to birthday parties and joined in groups while eating in the lunchroom. I began to learn the ropes from the "leaders" of the workforce, as opposed to the supervisors (big difference). Nobody knew I was making only a temporary stop in their world. As far as the rest of the workers at the plant were concerned, I was just another one of the guys collecting a paycheck; all the while, though, I was planning my escape to Europe and living this social experiment in the meantime. I was a college kid and this was part of my curriculum.

And I was learning. It didn't take me long to realize how forlorn, gloomy, and unfulfilling this life could be—how quickly one could get sucked into the fatalistic, perpetually disgruntled attitude on the line. Every conversation was a complaint about one aspect of life or another, and even the highly paid union workers took part in the rampant negativity. "My wife is a bitch, my boss is a dumb-ass, the company is greedy, my car is a junk, I've got a hangover"—these seemed to be the only topics of discussion among the workforce I had become part of. I missed talking about sports, arguing about politics, and hashing over the esoteric elements of philosophy and religion with the gang at Marquette. I missed the beer. I missed the coeds. I was coming to loathe this factory life I had found to be so fascinating at first.

I was impressionable, and I was getting sucked in fast. Within the culture of this factory, I discovered a sort of underworld that catered to nearly every vice and human depravity you'd find on the streets of a big city or even inside the walls of a prison. You could score almost any drug, legal or illegal. Everyone knew who had what, and people bought, sold, and used right there on the premises with only minimal concern about being caught. Since my job was to track all over the plant on my forklift, I knew almost everyone on the floor, and since my 12-hour shift spanned parts of two 8-hour shifts, I knew quite a few people. It wasn't long before I was turning down requests to deliver drugs from one area of the plant to another and from a person on one shift to one on another. I refused to take part in the black market.

There were women working there who would offer sexual favors in the back of the plant on every shift. Whether this was part of the underground commerce of the factory, I never knew. At first I was shocked when I went to the back to retrieve crates of resin that were kept locked in a special gated area and spotted the lewd acts being practiced. Before long I got as jaded as everyone else and just avoided the places where such adult behavior was going on. People were always drinking alcohol—usually out of fast-food cups, through straws—and somebody was always intoxicated. People punched other people's time cards to cover up for someone arriving late or leaving early; they treated equipment carelessly and wasted material unthinkingly, and I was shocked that there weren't more accidents in that plant. Management didn't trust the workers, the workers didn't trust the management, and few of the workers seemed to trust one another. Gradually, for me, it was becoming a very dark place.

Every morning I would get up at 5:30, shower, and walk across the street to the factory in the bitter cold before the sun was up. Then I would mount my forklift and schlep skids around all day, constantly playing catch-up from the night before. At 6 in the evening, when it was already dark, without having seen the sun once all day, I would walk back across the street to our boxy second-floor apartment in a gigantic complex, fitted out with hand-me-down furniture, a small television, a cheap stereo, and a bong. Without the bong, I would have realized much sooner how miserable this life was getting to be.

One night, after a dinner of boiled hot dogs and canned beans, Jimmy noticed I was becoming increasingly and uncharacteristically despondent. He was not one to pry into personal feelings (guys didn't do that), but he was always a great one to talk to. We had been through a lot of growing up together—he, along with Doug (another great lifelong friend), was there for my mom while I was off on my jaunt to Texas and both were there waiting when I returned home. I was there to comfort him after a big blowout with his dad by getting him a ticket to join a group of us at an Aerosmith concert at Comiskey Park. (Yeah, the one where the stands caught fire.) We played on the basketball and baseball teams together, chased a few girls, and truly cared about each other, not typical of relationships I'd had with other guys. Anyway, he eased his way into asking what was bothering me. I wasn't sure exactly until I started to talk: "I hate my job."

I was disillusioned by the factory and I was not content with my life. The thing is, Jimmy was always happy—and I mean *always*. "Jimmy, our life kind of stinks right now, let's face it. Don't you see it? We live in a crappy part of town, we both have menial jobs, and we have one car between us—yours. I want so much more than this," I said. "How come you're always so damn happy?"

I'll never forget his response, one that echoed in my mind again and again throughout my life whenever the feeling of discontent would pop up. "Well, Tim, it's not that I *never* get down, because I do. But whenever I *do*, I simply stop and think about all the things in my life that make me feel good, the things I feel lucky for. I guess the things I feel blessed about."

"Yeah, like what? A junky car? A shitty job? A grumpy roommate?" He laughed and looked at me almost sympathetically. "No, Timmy," he said. "For my parents, good friends like you, all the brothers and sisters that love me and that I love, our little apartment, the meal we just shared. And then always—in a very short time—I don't feel so bad about whatever is bothering me."

"That's *it?*" I asked. "You just *think* about good things?"

"Yep. It's really that simple—I just think about things that I'm grateful for and things that make me happy and then the bad stuff doesn't seem so bad anymore."

His "wisdom" (and life itself would teach me in time how wise it really was) seemed kind of stupid to me and didn't go very far in consoling me in that moment, but I'd known him long enough to know he really meant it. He was *always* happy. Even though his philosophy on life didn't appeal to me on that particular night, I knew it worked for him and I began to think a lot about it. But I wasn't one to merely think—I was more prone to action (sometimes *without* thinking), and soon I would take action about my situation.

I was getting an eye-popping slice of real life in the unedu-cated blue-collar world. Working without passion to collect a pay-check, complaining about my job, not liking the people I worked with very much, and losing sight of my future—I didn't like the person I was becoming at all. Spiritually, too, I was feeling lost. I had stopped going to Mass, and without even the rudimentary theology classes from college to keep me connected, I was drift-ing rapidly into indifference. I began smoking more, and I dis-covered the anesthetizing value of beer. Drinking and smoking was no longer a harmless college-boy thing to do for fun, it was a way to cope.

The longer I was away from school, the further my quest for spiritual meaning slipped from my consciousness. Seldom now did I think about religion, spirituality, or what the difference between the two might be. This topic felt esoteric and slightly frivolous when I was confined to earning a paycheck and fending off the poisonous negativity in the plant.

In early March the handler who normally worked on my days off went on vacation and I had to cover for him. After working 14 consecutive days from 6 a.m. until 6 p.m., I had had enough. I hadn't seen the sun for two weeks, and I heard that small voice inside me again, telling me to get free. This was a part of the "real world" I wanted no part of. I didn't even stop to consider how it might jeopardize my plans for Rome; I unceremoniously walked into the personnel office after I'd fulfilled my obligation to cover the vacation and quit on the spot. I walked out that dark and fro-zen evening and never returned.

EVERYBODY INTO THE POOL

I didn't have to worry about saving for Rome, because I quickly found a new job. I went from the dank, dark life of the factory to a swimming-pool company serving Chicago's wealthy North Shore. I spent the winter months at the factory experiencing how I didn't want to live and, once spring arrived, the next several months seeing how I did want to live.

Cleaning pools in the lush backyards of the suburban elite would give me a great sense of life's possibilities, and this too would serve me later in life. I saw how the other half lived. I saw the security and togetherness money could give a man with a family. I saw how radically different a home was without the worry of making ends meet—yet I also saw that the men who owned these large, beautiful homes were not too different from me. In these luxurious surroundings, I somehow felt at home.

At the plastic factory, I had hidden my plans to go to Rome. Now, everyone I got into a conversation with would hear about them, and instead of the resentment and teasing I would have had at the factory, I got encouragement and congratulations. Driving in my own company van from pool to pool, I had time to reflect and to think about my future again. I began to feel my enthusiasm return for what lay ahead.

My spirit was coming alive again as I shook off the abject negativity of the factory. The positive feedback I was getting about returning to school was good for my self-esteem, and I was reestablishing my connection to the voice inside, starting with the day I listened to it and quit the job at the factory. Many a successful man during that summer gave me encouragement and advice while I was working in his backyard opening his pool for the upcoming season, servicing a filter, or testing the chemicals in his water. I met with hardly any snobbery at all; it seemed that the axiom "the bigger they are, the nicer they are" was true. And seeing these people and their lives up close was instilling a motivation and aspirations for which I would otherwise have had no frame of reference. It was the "conceive" part of W. Clement Stone's famous maxim: "Whatever the mind of man can conceive and believe, it can achieve."

Soon it was August and nearly time to head off to Rome. I had never expected the kind of education I'd received in the time between the end of the fall semester of 1978 and the start of the fall semester of 1979, but it deserved a degree of its own. I had learned about the real world by working real jobs, but boy, was I ready to get back to searching for my answers in the academic world. Though I would someday take my own chance at the American Dream, I wanted to put that inevitable part of life off until I had better direction, more to offer, and the ability to command a decent wage. For now, it was time to get back to loftier ideals and a hell of a lot more fun. Working for a living could wait a while.

At this juncture of my journey, I found that:

- I had drifted farther from any spiritual connection than ever before. Did the real world strip us of our spiritual inclinations?

- Religion and spirituality might just be esoteric interests—not the stuff of real life.

- Life could be negative and very hard. I did not want to work in a factory my whole life.

- "The bigger they are, the nicer they are"—this maxim was true. Successful people seemed happy and generous.

- Other people's accomplishments inspired me. I wanted to emulate them.

- I was more anxious than ever to deepen my understanding of religion.

I had experienced my first "time out" from religious indoctrination of any kind. I had allowed the real world to pull my attention away from spiritual and religious matters, but at the same time, I was growing up. My education continued during my hiatus from academia as I learned a little about the "real world." I wasn't agnostic during this time; spiritually numb might be a better way to put it. And now I was ready to resume my lofty quest for Truth.

SIX

WHAT IS CHRISTIANITY?

FROM DEPOSIT TO DOCTRINE

Ask most Christian laypeople how their religion originated—who started it—and most will probably tell you it came straight from Jesus Christ, who was sent to establish a new covenant between mankind and God. That's certainly what I was taught to believe. Most of us were also taught that the Apostles were the authors of the Gospels, that the Bible contains no errors whatsoever, and that the Church doctrine that has come down to us through the centuries is the Truth just as Jesus revealed it. But it doesn't take a whole lot of sleuth work to discover that these are oversimplifications; these tidy little understandings are simply not the case. For example, if you ask a member of the clergy in just about any Christian denomination who wrote the four Gospels, he or she will certainly know that it *wasn't* the Apostles. That's a basic piece of information anyone with even a minimal biblical education would have. It makes one wonder why most rank-and-file believers don't have it as well.

The idea that the Gospels were penned by the Apostles is not a modern invention; one of the early Church Fathers, Justin Martyr, wrote of the New Testament in *The First Apology of Justin:* ". . . for the Apostles in the memoirs composed by them, which were called Gospels . . ." But the formation of the Church was not as straightforward as the Apostles simply memorializing their experiences and then spreading out to carry a message to the world based on specific instructions from Jesus. In the early days of the faith there were many interpretations of what "Christianity" was, and it took hundreds of years to even come close to a unified theology. Likewise, the Gospels took hundreds of years to be set down and settled on, and they were most certainly not written by Apostles. They were written by anonymous sources who never knew Jesus or met anyone who had. The doctrine of the Christian Church and the contents of the Bible were *decisions,* made by men far removed in time from the main characters and guided in many cases by motives of their own.

Society today (Christians included) is more critical in its thinking, more alert to inconsistencies and incongruities, than it was even a century ago, and biblical scholarship has advanced new ideas about the origins of canon and doctrine more in the last two hundred years than in the previous two thousand. But most ordinary Christians don't get the chance to examine their religion in this critical light. Scripture expert Bart Ehrman writes: "Scholars of the Bible have made significant progress in understanding the Bible over the past two hundred years, building on archeological discoveries, advances in our knowledge of ancient Hebrew and Greek languages in which the books of Scripture were written, and deep and penetrating historical, literary and textual analysis. This is a massive scholarly endeavor. Thousands of scholars in North America alone continue to do serious research in the field, and the results of their study are regularly and routinely taught, both to graduate students in universities and to prospective pastors attending seminaries in preparation for the ministry. Yet such views of the Bible are virtually unknown among the population at large. . . . As a result, not only are most Americans (increasingly) ignorant of the contents of the Bible, but they are also almost completely in the dark about what scholars have been saying about the Bible for the past two centuries."[1] Is it any wonder that more and more people "just don't feel right" about what they were taught as youngsters?

As we start to realize that we've been in the dark—and that this "revealed" religion may have gotten some significant retooling before it reached us—a new set of questions comes to light.

Did Jesus intend to start a new religion at all?

Who really wrote the Gospels?

*When, how, and on what basis were texts
chosen to form the New Testament?*

Who established the theological tenets of Christianity?

Did the secular, political, or pagan world impact Christian doctrine?

*Was Christianity the will of its namesake . . . a sacred conspiracy
of his small band of disciples . . . or preordained by God himself?*

The answers to questions like these, about the key decisions made very early in the life of Christianity that set its course for the centuries ahead, are especially important to those who struggle with doctrine as we inherit it today. For me, coming to understand better how the earliest conclusions of Christianity were drawn and how the core doctrine was developed helped to balance my *experience* of God with my *indoctrination* into the belief system.

THEOLOGY THROUGH THE GRAPEVINE

Jesus was an orator, not a writer; he left no written teachings, formal theology, or organizing principles for early leaders to use as a guide. For many decades after his death, Jesus' teachings and the story of his life were passed along by word of mouth. The very first people doing the telling were the actual witnesses to the ministry of Jesus—the Apostles. They began a tradition of orally testifying about Jesus and their stories were passed on through the human grapevine. In time, of course, these firsthand sources died out. The period from the Crucifixion to the death of the last apostle is called the Apostolic Era. This is important because when the time came to compile the New Testament hundreds of years later, one of the criteria for a text was how close to this era its author was thought to have lived.

Early Christianity was a fluid and developing theology. To say it *evolved* from the Apostles' original telling would not be overstating it. As the Apostles spread the word, others took it up and began to pass it along. The stories and sayings of Jesus made their way as "oral tradition" from town to town, from region to region, and from one generation to the next in the fluctuating way that stories are memorialized, susceptible to ever-changing interpretation. Furthermore, because early Christianity was outlawed by the Roman Empire and had to be practiced with some secrecy, oral transmission was the safer mode; written text increased the risk of exposure.

Gradually, written text began to pin the teachings of the emerging, evolving Church to paper and impede the natural evolution of oral tradition. Even so, for many years there was no standard of acceptable text and thus no authoritative theology to define Christianity. Various "churches" throughout its expanding sphere of influence began to adopt preferred "books" to use in their own communities, with each bishop approving or rejecting points of doctrine independent of the others. These early years were a time of diverse beliefs and theologies in the making; some ideas and texts prevailed and flourished and others were suppressed or banished.

The term *catholic* wasn't used in connection with Christianity until about 110 CE. The word, which means "universal," denoted a church that would be available to all, where all would be welcomed and accepted (as opposed to Judaism, which was intended for a "chosen people"). Later, as beliefs continued to diversify and adapt, *catholic* would take on a more formal meaning, defining a specific brand of orthodoxy.

Gradually, as the first decades passed into centuries, the Church began to conceive of itself as an institution and concern itself with matters of administration and hierarchy. Evangelizing became more about growing the size of the Church with sheer numbers of adherents and less about the salvation of the people being evangelized. The leaders became not only *teachers* of the new religion, but *protectors* of its theology. The administration of the institution demanded this: the theology needed to stop evolving and stabilize in order for a "catholic" or universal institution to take solid root.

COMPETING CREEDS

In time, of the divergent sects forming around their own theologies, three "branches" came to vie for influence: Orthodoxy, Gnosticism, and Marcionism.

Broadly speaking, Gnostics (from the Greek *gnosis,* "knowledge") believed that a person could achieve knowledge of God through knowledge of self. They believed that humans contained a degree of divinity within and that they, the Gnostics, held keys to unlocking it that the rest of humanity did not. One gained understanding, or *gnosis,* not by learning or studying, but by awakening to spiritual mysteries.

Marcionism, a school of thought formulated by the bishop Marcion in what is now Turkey, held that Jesus represented a complete break from the Jewish tradition. He was not the fulfillment of Jewish scripture; he was the son of a different God than the God of the Sinai in the Jewish text. The "new" God was a good God, unlike the punishing, angry God depicted in the Torah. The covenant of Jesus represented something totally new and not an extension of something very old. For this reason, the Torah was not part of the Marcion canon.

The Orthodox leaders needed both of these differing beliefs to disappear in order for the institution of the Church to take root. If man could come to a realization of God through his own innate knowledge, or *gnosis*—if God lived within each person— then the rationale for the institution was immediately threatened. And if Jesus was *not* a fulfillment of Scripture, if he was something new altogether—which contradicted the idea that Jesus fulfilled the prophecy of the Old Testament—the Church risked losing the core of its faithful, as the first followers of Jesus were mostly Jews who weren't prepared to discard Judaism. Orthodoxy states that Jesus came to start a religion and that the leaders of the Church gained their authority directly from Jesus via a line of succession that led back to Jesus through Peter. Further, since Jesus was in fact God, their authority was sacred, absolute, and unassailable. They were charged with converting the world to God's true church, the Holy Catholic (universal) Church, and any alternate belief system was a threat.

For the Orthodox Church to go from a persecuted secret society to the official religion of the Roman Empire, all the while fighting off theological challenges from within, it would need friends in high places. Some three hundred years after its initial deposit of faith, it found such a friend in Constantine the Great, a gifted politician and successful military leader who changed the course of its history forever.

THE EMPIRE CONVERTS

When Constantine came to power in Rome in 306 CE, the persecution of the Church was at its height and Christians were being slaughtered throughout the Empire. Legend has it that Constantine experienced a sudden and dramatic conversion that ended the persecution and made the Christian Church the official church of the Roman Empire. There is indeed some romance attached to the story that Constantine had a vision of a large cross in the sky and underwent a profound change of heart, and there is little doubt that without him the Church would not have enjoyed the reversal of fortune and rapid expansion throughout the civilized world that it did. The favor he bestowed on the Church, however, was due as much to political expediency as to personal beliefs. Constantine the politician saw tolerance of religion within the Empire as strategically useful. He made it law in 313 with the Edict of Milan, which, among other liberties it granted, outlawed mass executions of Christians. In reality, Constantine came to appreciate Christianity gradually throughout his life and likely didn't personally convert until many years after he authorized Christianity as the church of the Empire.

During the early part of Constantine's reign, there was no single doctrine to unify Christian churches, and disputes in the belief system were still rampant. Constantine saw the differences as detrimental to the political unity he sought within the Empire. When two leaders in Alexandria—Alexander, the bishop there, and Arius—had a major disagreement over the nature of Jesus, Constantine called some three hundred bishops to Nicaea, in what is now Turkey, to settle the dispute and forge a unified doctrine for the expanding religion. Constantine presided over what is considered the first ecumenical council in Church history, the Council of Nicaea in 325 CE. For the sake of unity, it was time to stop Christian theology from evolving once and for all.

The Council of Nicaea produced the declaration of faith known to this day as the Nicene Creed, which laid out the salient points of Christian belief and settled the controversy about the nature of Jesus. One side (Arius) argued that God had *created* Jesus and therefore Jesus' existence began at a *point in time;* the other side (Alexander) argued that Jesus *was* God and existed (with God) for *all time.* Alexander's side won and Jesus-as-God became official. In other words, this body *voted* to decide Jesus' true nature: *in 325 CE, the Council of Nicaea declared him to be God.*

Although clergy conducted the debate, Constantine played a large role in moving the body toward this conclusion. Constantine at the time was not yet converted, was not even a catechumen, and, in fact, had no training in Christianity. Constantine was likely a pagan at the time of the Council of Nicaea, yet his opening address to the bishops influenced the outcome of a theological debate that Church scholars had failed to settle on their own.

Defining the nature of Jesus was important politically as well as theologically. With the authority of God behind the message of Jesus, Orthodox theology became absolute truth. The Church, now the "official" church of the Roman Empire, gained the authority to declare other views heretical and wipe out any opposition. By 435 CE, it was legal for the Church to kill any heretic. To interpret the message of Jesus for oneself was not legal, and to question any doctrine of the Church was met not with dialogue or debate but with death. The evolutionary, expansive quality of the early Church was a thing of the past. The credo laid down in 325 CE remains today.

Constantine did ultimately convert to Christianity and was baptized by Eusebius, Bishop of Nicodemia, in 337 on his deathbed, years after he made Christianity legal and viable within the Roman Empire. Constantine strategically used the Church to gain political power and forge unity within the Empire. In turn, the Orthodox leaders made it very easy for him to accept the religion by granting him some power over shaping the doctrine and by adopting many Roman traditions. It's even possible that, perhaps to appease or appeal to Constantine, the theology of the Christian Church in that formative period assimilated some elements of the Romans' pagan beliefs. ("Perhaps" is the key word there. This possibility is worth considering, but it's not an attempt to disqualify the tenets of Christianity, just an invitation to keep an open mind.)

THE MYTH OF MITHRA

Constantine, with his military background, would certainly have known of the pagan god Mithra, who was worshipped as the "Protector of the Empire." The cult of Mithra probably originated in Persia (modern Iran) and its ancient pantheon, most likely from Zoroastrian roots. Soldiers returning from the East probably introduced this deity to Rome.

mental tenets of Mithra worship will be familiar to any-
even a passing acquaintance with Christian beliefs:

- Mithra was born on December 25 in a cave in the presence of
shepherds.

- Mithra was born of a virgin. (Virgin birth was also a relatively
common occurrence in Greek and Roman mythology.)

- Mithra performed miracles and was accompanied by 12 com-
panions.

- Mithra was believed to be a savior or messiah.

- Mithra rose from the dead three days after he died.

- Followers of Mithra were promised eternal life.

- The main feast honoring Mithra was tied to the spring equinox.

- Services to honor Mithra were performed by "fathers"; the chief
among them, Pater Patrum, or Father of the Fathers, lived in
Rome.

- The place of worship (temple) was built to look like a cave; the
main temple of Mithra was a cave on Vatican Hill.

It's easy to see why the Church might be a little "sensitive"
about Mithraism. And it's no surprise that most Christians, even
today, have never heard of Mithra. That's not to suggest, however,
that the Church doesn't have a comeback.

These "coincidences" in the tenets of Christianity and Mithraism, according to Church Fathers (specifically, Tertullian and Justin Martyr), may be explained in one of several ways. One is that these similarities are the work of the devil, Satan's heinous way of ridiculing and discrediting the truth of the Christian Church. By these lights, Satan must have known how the faith was going to arise and attempted to preempt it with this pagan imitation—"a diabolic mimicry by a prescient Satan," in the Church Fathers' words. Another explanation is that Mithraism is a cosmic anticipation, or foreshadowing, of Christianity, but without the evil influence of Satan. Still another explanation is that Christianity borrowed some of its most basic theology from Mithraism to make it easier to convert the pagan Constantine. After all, it would be logical for an emperor with a military past like Constantine's to align himself with a god believed to be a protector of the Roman Empire. We can see why he would not want to alienate this deity. In fact, Constantine took great care not to alienate any deities; he was politically astute even with the pantheon that made up the Roman mythology. (He took care not to agitate the Christian God either.)

Why would the early Fathers of the Church consider adopting some aspects of a pagan religion to formulate their own tenets? Perhaps they did nothing of the sort, but if they did, the rationale would most certainly be political and not theological. They didn't need any more help formulating theology, they needed to gain acceptance from the Roman Emperor in order to survive another generation. If Christianity had an air of familiarity, wouldn't it be easier to "sell" to an emperor who was looking for political and religious unity to begin with?

The fact is that once Constantine legalized Christianity, it spread like a wildfire on a windy day in a drought. The right to use the Roman roads alone advanced the faith in ways that would otherwise have taken centuries. Add the right to kill off any opposition, backed by the force of the Empire, and the fledgling religion was rapidly becoming a world power in wealth, might, and influence. This may be a cynical view of the fathers of Christianity, but their shrewdness should not be underestimated. After all, they had no problem extinguishing any threat to their own authority through execution, so what's a little bit of "story development"?

In regard to Mithra, either God foreshadowed events of His son's arrival through the ancient story, Satan stepped out front of the Incarnation and used a pagan cult to ridicule God, or the Church Fathers were extremely savvy men who justified the means by the end. Any of these stories is fascinating, only one is true.

GOSPEL TRUTH

One thing is clear: the content of the Christian *religious belief system* arose through a series of human decisions made according to human agendas. Does the same hold true for the content of its *sacred texts?*

Let's start with what the Catechism of the Catholic Church says about the origins of Scripture: "God inspired human authors of the sacred books. To compose the sacred books, God chose certain men who, all the while he employed them in this task, made full use of their own faculties and powers so that, though he acted in them . . . they consigned to writing whatever he wanted written and no more."[2] Effectively, the Christian Bible, which includes both the New and Old Testaments, is said to be authored by God, written through inspired human hands. And this belief about divine inspiration leads by logical extension to the doctrine of inerrancy. If the Bible is the Word of God, it cannot contain any errors whatsoever, since God does not lie and is never wrong.

Divinely inspired or not, it was men of faith, not historians of facts, who wrote the New Testament. More than likely, these men wrote from a particular point of view and these books were written for specific theological purposes. In the early days of the Church, there were dozens, if not hundreds, of gospel accounts, each with its own slant on Christianity. The four canonical Gospels are the ones that made the cut. (More on that in a minute.)

The New Testament consists of 27 books in four basic categories: the four Gospels, which tell the story of Jesus' life, ministry, death, and resurrection; the Acts of the Apostles, which account for the early formation of the church; the Epistles, or letters of instruction and inspiration written to early churches; and, finally, prophecies that tell of the future. The Gospel attributed to Mark is thought to be the earliest of the four, probably dating to between 60 and 70 CE, at least 30 to 40 years after Jesus died. Mark was followed by Matthew, penned between 70 and 80 CE, and Luke, between 80 and 90 CE. The gospels of Luke and Matthew appear to use some material from Mark and to derive at least some of their information from a lost text called *Q* (for the German *quelle*, meaning "source"). *Q*, thought to have been written five to ten years before Mark, would have been the first written record of Jesus' life; before that, it was all word of mouth. John's Gospel was the last to be written, probably in the 90s or early 100s CE (though some historians date its writing as late as 150 CE).

Tradition says that those four eyewitnesses to Jesus' life wrote the Gospels—this is what most ordinary Christians were taught and believe—but Bible experts, including nearly all clergy, Catholic or Protestant, know what the average Christian does not: that Matthew, Mark, Luke, and John most certainly did not write these accounts. The original texts were written in Greek, but the followers of Jesus spoke Aramaic; they were agrarian laborers, fishermen, and tax collectors who most likely did not read, let alone write. The authors of the Gospels were talented, educated writers, probably with experience or training.

Also, none of the Gospel writers actually claim to be eyewitnesses to Jesus. With the exception of some language at the very end of the Gospel of John, they write in the third person, not the first: *Jesus spoke to the disciples*, not *Jesus spoke to us.* It is likely that the Gospels were written by educated believers who didn't know Jesus and never met an original disciple.

CONSIDER THE SOURCE

If the four Apostles did not write the Gospels that bear their names, how did they get the bylines? In my 13 years in the newspaper business, I learned early on that one of the basic tenets of credible reporting is attribution. A news story that is not attributed to a source is more of an opinion than "news." For example, when a reporter wants to introduce a fact into a news account, he or she should *not* simply place the fact into the story without stating clearly where it comes from. Stories with "anonymous sources" are problematic, and as the publisher, it was very rare that I would allow them in our paper.

A good editor wants readers to trust the reporting and knows that each fact needs attribution to some identifiable source. Experience taught me *anonymous* was rarely reliable. Usually, I found that when sources wanted to remain anonymous, they were either not telling the truth or they had an agenda—and often, if we worked a little harder and dug a little deeper, we could confirm the fact they offered through another source that *was* reliable.

The earliest "editors" of the Gospel text must have agreed that anonymity undermined credibility. Most scholars today agree that the original texts of the New Testament were originally anonymous and remained so for many years. Only long after the Gospels were written did the Church leaders involved in assembling the canon "attribute" these writings to identifiable sources whom readers would know: Matthew, the tax-collector disciple; Mark, a close associate of the Apostle Peter; Luke, a student of Paul, and John, the Apostle of Jesus. All of these sources had an acceptable degree of relationship to the Apostolic Era. The texts were attributed to them for the same reason a newspaper editor seeks attribution—so that the story would have the authority of independent truth, told by an eyewitness. Would you rather read an eyewitness account of a major event from someone who was actually there or a story that was passed along, three or four times removed from the eyewitness? Think of the difference between hearing stories about the Civil War from a *student* of the Civil War versus hearing them from a *veteran.*

If newspaper editors attributed the way the Gospel editors did, by arbitrarily using names of credible and powerful people as sources to bolster their stories, it wouldn't be journalism anymore. (It would be more like blogging!) And they would certainly lose their jobs.

CANON FODDER

These Gospels were four out of dozens, even hundreds, of texts that laid out some portion of Jesus' life and message. Several other texts purported to be written by apostles as well. Thomas, Peter, James, and Mary Magdalene all have gospels written in their names. How is it that these four accounts of Jesus' life became the canon? How was it determined that God inspired only four?

The Church father Bishop Irenaeus, of Lugdunum (Lyons) in present-day France, in 185 CE declared the Gospels of Matthew,

Mark, Luke, and John to be the volumes approved for Christians. Other narratives of Jesus' life were circulating that claimed to be written by other disciples—there were at least 30 such accounts at the time—but the theology they espoused was declared heresy by Irenaeus and others, and they were disallowed and ordered destroyed. The four that contained the acceptable theological points were anonymous, hence the need for attribution to authoritative figures.

What makes these four orthodox or *inspired* and the others heresy? The Catechism claims that God inspired the New Testament. Since there were so many testaments to choose from, wouldn't it be accurate to say that they were *divinely selected* also? How do we know today that Irenaeus, and others after him, chose the correct texts? To distinguish inspired writing from heretical writing, wouldn't they need divine inspiration themselves?

Settling on Church orthodoxy was a process, and a profoundly human one. There was nothing clear-cut or unanimous about what was true (authored by God) and what was heretical. So many texts came to be produced that at some point it became necessary to cull them—to declare some authoritative and others not. The *official* criterion used was a concept called *Apostolic Authority:* the more directly derived a text was from an Apostle or someone approved of by an Apostle, the more reliable it was. This is why Irenaeus attached the names of Jesus' disciples to the anonymous accounts that best suited his ends, and why, even to this day, the common Christian believes the Apostles wrote the Gospels.

WHAT DID HE MEAN TO SAY?

The formation of the New Testament was a subjective business at best, and all the more so because so much is lost (or inadvertently gained) in translation. This is because translation opens the door to the interpreter's point of view, and each point of view may contain an agenda. The original texts of the books of the New Testament were written in Greek. This means that the first written texts about the teachings of Jesus were *already* translations, as Jesus spoke Aramaic. Also, before there was agreement on which texts to use and in which form, Scripture consisted of literally thousands of individual written documents, and each new "copy" introduced changes, either by mistake or by design.

There are no surviving original texts of the New Testament, so there is no way to run a line of comparison from the original to a current edition to check for accurate interpretations. Countless copies were made by hand over the centuries before printing presses, and probably not one is an exact replica of the one it was supposedly copying—and that's just human error. How far from the original texts are the ones we read today? Bart Ehrman suggests, "There are more differences in our manuscripts than there are words in the New Testament."[3]

So I ask again—how do we know that the "inspired" texts God intended were actually the ones "selected"? And can we reasonably believe that the versions that have survived into our era passed through the human filter of rewriting and reinterpreting to yield an inerrant Word of God? It stretches the imagination to suppose that what we have today is what God intended more than 20 centuries ago.

Jesus left no clear instruction on forming a church, no tenets of theology, no written lessons. Decisions made by men many years after Jesus set the patterns for the Church that survive today. Men selected the contents of the Bible, which we are taught is the inerrant Word of God. And the tenets of Christianity, which we are taught as God's truth, were formed in light of the political realities of the Roman Empire. Orthodoxy won on both counts, as it managed to eliminate any texts that offered a differing theology and to gain authority from Rome to eliminate any challenge to itself.

It is quite possible that the early Christian Church that survived and flourished was the sect that had the best *human* leadership, not the most direct divine mandate. The Orthodox faction of early Christianity made all the right moves to rise above the competition. (Or maybe this shows they *were* inspired.)

Christians are expected to believe God authored the New Testament as divinely inspired humans took dictation. And yet it took hundreds of years to select the books to be included, and many were left out. If we had chosen different Gospels, what would Christianity be?

I think it serves us well to understand some of the basic facts of how Christianity came to be the way we have it passed to us today. It allows us to step over the barriers of what we were taught (the dogma of inerrancy, the notion of God's one true Church) and draw our own conclusions. It is obvious that Jesus left no specific instructions about who or what he was or how the Church should be built. It took several hundred years to codify answers. If it took the leaders of the Church, starting with those who knew Jesus personally, three hundred to four hundred years to devise the theology of Jesus, don't feel bad if you need some time to reflect upon it for yourself.

SEVEN

THE DEAL

When in Rome...

I arrived in Rome on a warm, dry August afternoon. I was tired from the long flight in my three-piece suit, and I became a bit bewildered when the first Italians I saw upon exiting the plane at Fiumicino Airport were soldiers in full uniform armed with compact machine guns. I had a vague understanding of the terrorist problems in Italy at that time—the Brigate Rosse, or Red Brigades, were striking at the "imperialist" state with robberies, kidnappings, and killings—but I'd never seen a gun before. I was surprised by how anxious the sight of them made me. I wondered aloud to no one in particular, "What if one of those goes off?"

Between the temperature and the anxiety I felt over the guns, I began to sweat through my suit jacket. I was relieved when I spotted a person holding a Loyola sign. He helped me find a taxi that would take me to the school. I had made it across parts of two continents and the Atlantic Ocean on my own; now I was grateful to have someone take responsibility for my well-being and guide me the rest of the way.

My year in Rome would prove to be one of acute growth spackled with intense sensory experiences and powerful spiritual events. I arrived in Rome as, well, a clod. I was a Midwestern kid without much in the way of sophistication, and I didn't really understand how to travel; I had been on an airplane only one time before, an hour-long flight to Detroit. I knew little of Europe, and all I knew of Italy was what I had read in travel guides that summer. I don't think I fit the description of the classic "ugly American"; I think that moniker is reserved for those who travel to Europe as a status symbol, something to brag about at the country club, who get irked when the waiter in Paris doesn't speak English well enough or give them the same deferential treatment they may get at that country club. I surely wasn't one of those; I was just woefully uninformed—or perhaps comically uninformed would be a better way to describe my preparedness for European travel. I was the classic portrait of an "ignorant American."

Being young, I adapted quickly. The first few weeks were laughable and often embarrassing as I tried to fit in, but it didn't take long to get acclimated and to understand that young travelers are part of the European landscape. I was a goofy kid from Chicago, but I wasn't alone—there were plenty of goofs to go around, some from the East Coast, some from the West Coast, and some from the Midwest just like me. About half the kids were from affluent homes and well schooled in the art of Continental travel. I was not among that group; I would have to learn by experience, without being taught. That suited me just fine.

PASTA IN A PINCH

Loyola's campus was housed in a former convent atop Monte Mario, the highest point in Rome. The echoey halls with their marble floors were cool and refreshing after my sweaty journey. Kids were arriving alone or in small groups as I began to settle into my room—small and basic, as you'd expect from a convent— and after about two or three hours of unpacking and bullshitting with other guys, it was time to head to the cafeteria to eat our first meal of pasta and moon rocks, incredible home-baked rolls of soft fresh bread in a hard crust exterior that would become a staple of backpack fare. It was the first of hundreds of pasta meals we would eat together when we weren't exploring the Continent or visiting one of the hundreds of great *ristoranti* of Rome.

During that first meal together, I and a few other clods got to discussing what we "knew" about Italian culture. Two particular aspects seemed to preoccupy the conversation, topics that you wouldn't be surprised to hear being discussed in a cafeteria back in Milwaukee: burping and butts. Burping as in a noisy release of air via the mouth, and butts as in the gluteus maximus of the human female.

First, we discussed the fine art of belching. One of the social geniuses at the table confidently explained that in Italy, to belch after a fine meal stated in no uncertain terms that you had enjoyed the meal, that you had eaten your fill, and, further, that you enjoyed and appreciated the cook's effort. It was an auditory accolade to the meal preparer, an appropriate and socially acceptable recognition of a culinary triumph. To the rest of us 19- and 20-year-old clods this seemed reasonable and, I thought, very European. As halfwit boys are apt to do when engaged with a pack of other halfwits, we tested the theory after eating the best dorm meal we had ever experienced. The starchy, tasteless food we were served in the dorms back home was a memory now; we were being treated to authentic Italian cuisine and we wanted to express our appreciation in the most Italian way. So after we finished, a burp-fest broke out as each clod tried to outdo the others' "compliments," regaling the cafeteria crew with our symphony of adulation. The disgusting noises that would have prompted our mothers to thump our heads just made the Italian women who manned the cafeteria laugh. They had obviously seen this routine before. From our point of view, the compliment had registered; burping was acceptable in Italy. Cool.

After dinner, the dorm was cluttered with late-arriving students, so we went out into the courtyard to smoke cigarettes and heckle the newcomers struggling with trunks and backpacks as their taxis dropped them at the gates of the school property. Conversing aimlessly about nothing, as clods are wont to do, we resumed our discussion of Italian customs, and the new aspect of cultural convention that we hit on was even more interesting than burping in public. One of the clods explained to the rest of us that another acceptable compliment in Italy was to pinch a woman's butt. How sophisticated, how *very* Italian.

Since our compliments to the cafeteria crew had hit the mark, we couldn't wait to offer up more blandishments to the rest of the female population of Rome. Three of us clods were soon on a bus heading for the Piazza Navona, and one particular dolt was heading for disaster.

DO AS THE ROMANS DO

Eventually, the ancient Piazza Navona, with its famous Baroque fountain in the middle of a first-century Roman circus, its outdoor cafes and pasticcerias serving delectable *dolci,* its roving portrait artists and lively street theater, would be way too touristy for the cool American students we'd become, but for a first night's foray into the Roman evening it made a perfect destination. It was an uncomplicated bus ride from the school, and we were anxious to see the city, so shortly after sunset a few of us clods decided to venture out on our own into the hot August night.

As the bus wound its way down the streets of Monte Mario, we started speculating about who was going to "pinch some Roman ass." My companion idiots turned to the chief idiot of the group— me—and dared me to make the first move. As a natural leader, I thought this appropriate, and anyway, I seldom passed on a dare. I began watching for a likely candidate.

I didn't have long to wait before a beautiful and exotic woman sauntered onto the bus. She was wearing a sleeveless white gauzy dress that was sexy and revealing but not in the least promiscuous. She had blonde hair, a dark complexion, high heels that matched her dress, and a sultry swagger that commanded any healthy male to take notice (and a 19-year-old American nitwit to gawk). *A true Roman goddess,* I thought, *one worthy of the highest form of compliment.* She was curvy in all the right curvy kinds of places, and when she flashed a brilliant toothy smile past her considerable yet beautiful "Roman" nose, I took it as an invitation.

This very sophisticated woman, probably in her mid-30s, meandered to the middle of the nearly empty bus and reached up to grip the handrail directly above my head, revealing the truth of another Italian myth—an unshaven blonde armpit. She didn't take a seat but instead posed, statue-like, right in front of me and smiled right through me. I'm fairly sure I was in a trance.

I snapped out of it and considered the circumstances very carefully, using the stupid male logic of the hormonally deranged. Why did she choose to stand right in front of me on an empty bus? Was it an invitation to grab my first Roman keister? I hesitated only momentarily before I stood up, reached out, and grabbed a considerable handful of the voluptuous derriere.

The squeal of indignation was unmistakable; luckily, I ducked in time to avoid the snazzy valise she swung at my head. She turned and gave me a fearsome look of outrage, and I sensed something had gone terribly awry. Did I do it wrong? What about my salutation did she misunderstand? Could it be she wasn't Italian? Then I heard some commotion in the back of the bus and I noticed two wiry young Italian guys moving toward me with an unmistakable look of righteous fury in their eyes. They were yelling and pointing at me, and though I didn't understand one word, I fully understood their intent: they were coming to the goddess's defense and I was about to get tag-teamed by two paisanos. When I looked over at my two American acquaintances (clods not yet friends) and saw they were staring straight ahead, hands serving as blinders to the action in the aisle, I knew I was on my own.

I jumped out the open middle door of the bus just before the two do-rights reached me. Luckily, the bus wasn't traveling all that fast. As I looked back, I could see the paisanos shouting at me from the door I'd just jumped from; I could tell they didn't really want to jump off, so I was safe for the time being. When the bus stopped about 75 yards ahead of me and nobody got off, I felt a little safer. I walked up to that bus stop, waited about 15 minutes for the next bus, and continued alone to the Piazza Navona.

Small world! The reaction I got that night in Rome was the same as I would have gotten had I grabbed some poor innocent booty on the El in Chicago. Butt pinching in Italy was an urban legend, much like burping—and if it ever was in vogue, it certainly wasn't acceptable behavior for a young foreign lummox on public transportation.

SPANTALIAN LESSONS

That weekend, school still hadn't begun, we had a couple of days to explore Rome, and I was ready for my first foray outside the city. A few kids were planning a day trip to a beach outside of Rome and I decided to go along. It was a gloriously sunny day and some of the girls had packed lunches of cheese, prosciutto, and moon rocks from the cafeteria. We boys brought some wine and cans of Heineken. We all felt so sophisticated.

When we got to the beach and staked our little claim of sandy real estate, I noticed a rather pudgy elderly woman without a top to her bathing suit. Not exactly the goddess I'd seen on the bus just a few nights before, but a definite signal that I wasn't in Kansas anymore. Then we realized that even the younger and less paunchy were also sans tops. Never mind Oz—was I in Heaven? Everyone was topless except the coeds in our group, but despite the wine and the Heineken, their tops remained. Meanwhile, between the snickering and the gawking, everyone on the beach that Saturday could tell that the Americans had invaded—American clods.

Soon we got acclimated and began to meld with the Roman culture a little less obtusely. Most of the time it was obvious we were Americans, but as we learned to blend in, we became accepted foreign students, of which there were many in Rome. We were all required to take an accelerated course in Italian aimed at making us conversant as fast as possible. I quickly realized that Italian and Spanish constructions were similar and some of the vocabulary was recognizable, and it wasn't too long before I was speaking my own hybrid language. I called it Spantalian. I was quickly communicating with cabbies and waiters, as it seemed most all of them understood Spantalian. We stopped hanging around tourist areas like Piazza Navona and began to frequent clubs in Trastevere, where real Romans lived and played.

We went to nightclubs with live music where the bands distributed bongo drums, tambourines, and other percussion instruments to us so we could participate in the music. From Zodiaco, a hip neighborhood bar on Monte Mario, we could see the whole city spread out at our feet. At the end of an evening out we almost always ended up behind a bakery near the campus, buying world-class munchies from the back door.

There were about two hundred of us at the Loyola Rome Center (today called the John Felice Rome Center), divided nearly evenly between boys and girls. It was an intimate setting with dorm rooms, classrooms, cafeteria, lounges, and chapel all under one roof. The horseshoe-shaped building surrounded a courtyard that was the main congregating area for students to mingle and smoke. The school was run by a dour priest who acted as though he was serving a sentence in this remote outpost of academia. The faculty, however, seemed as happy to be in Rome as the students were and treated their time there as a sort of sabbatical. They were generally carefree, without the seriousness most professors seemed to have back in the States. The professors who taught my theology classes worked for the Vatican and were experts in their field.

These professors did much more than teach *religion*. Most of them had a very philosophical approach to theology and were motivated to stir up controversy about what we had been taught about Catholicism to that point. They actually *wanted* us to be cynical and to question—to a point. I remember making Father Pierre Riches—the pastor of a Catholic parish in Rome, born a Jew in Alexandria, Egypt—chuckle a little when I submitted a paper outlining the three "mistakes" Jesus made during his lifetime. Although he had initially provoked my thinking in that direction, he was very quick to point out that Jesus was God and that "mistakes" on his part were not possible. He had set me up. Father John Long (aka Long-and-Boring) worked at the Vatican Office for Ecumenism and taught an overly optimistic class focusing on the "pending return" of Protestant churches to Rome. We learned that Rome was willing to forgive when the Protestants were willing to forget. And many of our classes met at some of Rome's most cherished historic sites—how about an art class in the Vatican Museum or the Sistine Chapel? A morning bus trip to Florence to visit David in the Uffizi? Or an archeology class in the Coliseum or the Forum?

I relish many experiences from that year. The small campus on Monte Mario would serve as base camp for student expeditions throughout Europe, Africa, and the Middle East. There were late nights cruising Rome on my moped, circling the Vatican Obelisk at 2 a.m. (also on my moped), and evenings just hanging around drinking Heineken in Renaldo's, the coffee shop and snack bar in the basement of the school.

But there were also two powerful incidents that together changed the course of my life.

UPON THIS ROCK

The first experience was one that many visitors to Rome share to this day. The Scavi (the word in Italian literally means "excavations") are archeological explorations of an ancient necropolis located under Saint Peter's Basilica in Vatican City—a city of the dead where wealthy pagans entombed deceased relatives in "rooms" and "homes." In these spaces, the dead could pursue their new life in the otherworld. Several hundred years after the Apostle Peter was executed, Constantine had his remains moved to the necropolis atop Vatican Hill in Rome. Peter was martyred in Rome, as legend has it, after encountering the resurrected Jesus on the Appian Way as he was fleeing Nero's prosecution. Upon meeting Jesus, who was heading *into* Rome, Peter asked where he was going. Jesus replied that he was going to Rome to be crucified.

This reply, the tradition goes, prompted Peter to return to Rome to face his own crucifixion. Because he claimed to be unworthy to die in the same manner as Jesus, he was accommodated and crucified upside down.

Peter, the first leader of the Christian Church, demonstrated a very human tendency to waffle between skepticism and faith, for which Jesus seemed to chide him both during his mortal life and after the Resurrection. It was Peter who joined Jesus for a little stroll upon the Sea of Galilee, at first buoyed by faith only to be undone by uncertainty and a sudden plunge. On the night Jesus was betrayed by Judas, Peter bragged of his unconditional love for Jesus, only to deny him three times, as Jesus himself predicted. Jesus, in a bit of wordplay, changed his follower's original name from Simon to Peter, which comes from the Latin *petra* or "rock," saying, "You are Peter, and upon this rock I will build my church."[1]

Just a couple of weeks into the semester, my archeology class went on a tour of the Scavi. As a young priest led us deeper and deeper into the excavation, I began to get excited and a little emotional. I kept pestering the priest about what we would see at the end, and he kept imploring me to be patient and not spoil the climax for the other students. I thought we might be going to see the bones of Saint Peter. I was right. There, deep underground, in a dim, low-slung passage under the nave of the church, in a pagan cemetery beneath the very seat of Christianity, where the pivotal convert Constantine stashed the bones of the Church's first leader, I deeply felt the personal and poignant implications for my search for Truth.

In that moment, in a rush of recognition, the Scripture I was taught intersected with my own intimate experience in a most tangible way. The words Jesus had said to Peter—*you are the rock*—came alive. The way the Scavi unfolds makes it clear that throughout the centuries after Peter's martyrdom, Rome underwent a number of transformations. For the Basilica to actually rest upon the bones of "the rock" was truly a prophecy only God could have made. At least, that was how I saw it.

What did this mean for my personal quest? Once again, Apostolic Succession took on an overpowering and binding sense of truth I couldn't deny or dismiss. Suddenly, the metaphor Jesus used about Peter became historically tangible as well as privately observable. The sheer impact of the physical manifestation over-powered me. Here I was, crouching under this elaborate and sig-nificant building, the capital of Catholicism, which in turn was resting directly atop Peter, the rock.

Whew! Heady stuff! And it allowed me to overlook many of my other questions. I felt connected to Jesus through this building. This became more than a belief; it was distinctly experiential. It was physical *and* spiritual.

I had my answer. Although I still had problems with many doc-trinal issues, and with the behavior of the Church throughout his-tory as well, I couldn't argue with the significance of this direct line to Jesus. I rationalized again that no matter how corrupt the Church was, it was corrupted entirely by the nature of man and not through any fault of its "founder." What Jesus had initiated on earth, man could not cease, especially not this young man. If Jesus did in fact come to start a church—and at the time I had no alter-native opinion—I could accept the conduct of the Church if only because it literally was the fulfillment of Jesus' prophecy of build-ing upon this rock. This was bigger than my simpleminded differ-ences with doctrinal issues and human shortcomings. Apostolic Succession was the reason I had decided to continue to educate myself about Catholicism, and it remained the rock upon which I would base my decision to stay.

A DEAL WITH THE DIVINE

The second experience was much more private, as it took place in the solitude of my dorm room. Some time had passed since the Scavi incident and I had settled into the routine of school. Typically, I would attend classes in the morning, eat a lunch of pasta and salad, and then walk to a newsstand several blocks from school in the affluent neighborhood of Monte Mario, which was home to diplomats, politicians, and other prominent families. I began the habit of reading the *International Herald-Tribune* from cover to cover every afternoon before taking a short nap or finishing my day of classes. In the late afternoon, we would often play pickup basketball games on the red clay tennis court behind the school. Then, after showering the red dust out of my pores, it would be time for dinner: more pasta. Actually, we had pasta at every meal, and instead of getting sick of eating it so frequently I became almost addicted to it—I still love pasta.

After dinner on this particular evening, I went back to my room to relax for a little while. There was no TV, no stereo, none of the amenities of a typical dorm room back in Milwaukee. Our rooms were sparse: bed, desk, and chair, and that was it.

I was becoming sort of a night owl, probably because of the naps in the afternoon, and I wasn't ready to turn in. I decided to peruse the Bible I had just bought for one of my classes. I opened it randomly and started reading the Gospel of John. As I was reading, it happened.

The Scavi experience was religious and cognitive; a rational "aha" moment, it was an intellectual discovery that evoked emotion, but the experience was not spiritual in nature. The connection I was able to make between biblical history and the present-day Church was important at the time because it offered some answers

I thought I was seeking; it helped to tighten the story of my religion. But the experience in my room on this night was decidedly not intellectual; it was spiritual, ethereal, even though I wouldn't have used those words at the time. At the time I probably thought it too was a religious experience because it gave me a new understanding of the divine presence I had been trained to call God.

During my reading of John, I closed my eyes and entered into a state I had never experienced before. I did not fall asleep. I was not dreaming, I didn't lose consciousness, but I wouldn't say I wasn't in an altered state of some sort either. I didn't know at the time what to call it, and even today I am reluctant to label it. Maybe it was what Eastern spirituality calls *satori;* I don't know, but I don't necessarily doubt it. I don't know how long this episode lasted; it was longer than a few seconds, but probably not more than 10 or 15 minutes. When it passed and I opened my eyes, the room looked entirely different—brighter in some way. My vision seemed clearer and colors looked more vivid. I wasn't hallucinating or seeing things that weren't there; the things that *were* there were just brighter, clearer, and somehow more visible. I reread the passage from John that I had been reading when I entered that state and was amazed at the new understanding I had of it. "'I tell you most solemnly, unless a man is born from above, he cannot see the kingdom of God.' Nicodemus said, 'How can a grown man be born? Can he go back into his mother's womb and be born again?' Jesus replied: 'I tell you most solemnly, unless a man is born through water and the Spirit, he cannot enter the kingdom of God: what is born of flesh is flesh; what is born of the Spirit is spirit. Do not be surprised when I say: You must be born from above.'"[2]

Suddenly I understood with certainty that a person could come to communion with God from *within.* That's what Jesus was really saying: the connection to Spirit was already there in every person, available through an internal channel that was separate from the institution of religion. It didn't feel like a rejection of Church teaching at the time; it felt like this experience added something *on top of* my belief. I received an insight that the religion was standing on the path toward God. I did not yet perceive that the Church might be *blocking* the path, but I knew somehow that it was not the destination.

I felt a force of Spirit take hold of me with an incredible and unexplainable sense of oneness. In those moments, the duality and separation I had been sensing for many years consolidated into a sense of unity with a Spirit I had been trained to call God. At once, instantly, my fear and foreboding about God evaporated. I clearly felt the infinite benevolence that God must be. I didn't suddenly acquire faith—I had always had faith. This was a *knowing*, much different from hoping or trusting. Faith morphed into an *experience* of belief. There was a sudden joy in knowing I didn't have to look for God anymore; He was always within, ever accessible, constantly listening and willing to speak to me. I also knew, without being able to put it into words, that nothing would ever be the same as it was before this happened. In a flash, I saw my future laid out before me and it was good.

Without any tangible basis for such knowledge, I knew my life was destined for a specific task and that it would have to do with the very experience I had just had. This knowledge, this new understanding, was a responsibility, and at some point in the future I would be guided by this newfound indwelling of Spirit to take it on.

It was so elementary that it was downright funny, an inside joke between God and me. Here I was in the middle of Rome, the seat of Catholicism, studying this massive worldwide institutional belief system with centuries of dogma and tradition, seeking answers to complex and high-flown questions about my relationship to the

Divine, only to be given insight from within. In a rush of overwhelming understanding, I knew the Church was a man-made institution that could not deliver a man to where God really dwelt.

I knew that God existed *in me*. And I knew something else: I also became certain during that spiritual interlude that I would become financially successful enough to quit working at a young age. I would be put in a position to share this experience with others, and soon.

There was no question whatsoever in my mind that my trip to Rome had succeeded. I would continue to study theology, but it would never again look or feel the same. From this new perspective, I began to really look at Church history and doctrine with a more critical eye. At the same time, I knew I had a future of financial success waiting for me, early exit included. It was hard to take school seriously after that. Perhaps I should have taken this as a cue to major in business or something, but I didn't feel that was necessary for my future to unfold successfully. I didn't need a college degree. I was *destined* to become rich and there wasn't anything in the world, not even my own ignorance or arrogance, that could stop it.

I began to refer to this experience as The Deal. That may seem a little crass today, but that was my point of view. It wasn't very complicated, either: God would make me rich at a young age, and then I would tell the world where he was hiding. The Deal would guide me through the rest of my life. It would influence my decisions and allow me to approach life's challenges without doubt or fear of the outcome. Troubles and triumphs alike would be handled by the "higher" power I had found inside of me.

Not long afterward, I began attending Mass in Rome every day. Mass, however, was not the same as it had been before The Deal. The quiet darkness of the late afternoon service in the beautiful round chapel on the ground floor of the old convent became a sanctuary for reflection and "conversation" with the Spirit dwelling inside. The familiar cadence and rhythm of the Mass made the perfect background noise for getting lost in this bliss of communing with Spirit. It was in that little chapel, sitting in the back pew, that I started to see the view of my life take shape with the clarity gained from the experience in my dorm room.

From this period on, I would look at events in my life more and more through a spiritual lens. I didn't exactly make an overt attempt to see things more metaphysically, but after that night in my dorm room, I began to hear the voice of Spirit within me in every situation. The rest of my time in Rome was full of adventure, lots of travel and lots of fun, but I never escaped the new point of view I'd gained that night; I didn't really have a choice in the matter. Was I getting smarter? More aware? Was I still a clod?

I left Rome with some powerful tools and a newfound confidence about the results my life would produce:

- I *experienced* the presence of a benevolent being in a very personal way. I had crossed a barrier, moved beyond belief in dogma and doctrine. Once I experienced God, I sensed things would never be the same.

- I understood that religion was not the path to God—that every person had the innate potential to connect with the Divine.

- At the same time, I became more comfortable with Catholicism because my mind was able to grasp firsthand the linkage between Jesus, the Church, and me. It cemented my trust in Apostolic Succession.

- I entered into a pact—The Deal—that would become the source I returned to again and again for direction in my life.

- I concluded I didn't need a degree to move ahead in the world.

- I wanted to know more about Jesus.

In the excitement of my Roman revelations, what was lost on me was the obvious disconnect between my experience in the Scavi and The Deal. One affirmed the Church's direct link to Jesus and the other rejected religious institutions in favor of spiritual experience. How could I have missed the irony? I was clearly not as smart as I was beginning to think I was.

But I sure had come a long way from that first night of burping and butt pinching.

EIGHT

WHAT IS THE TRINITY?

The Math behind the Mystery

For Christians trying to fully grasp the teachings of their belief system and come to a deeper understanding of God, the doctrine of the Trinity is one of the thorniest. "If you deny the Trinity you will lose your soul," the saying goes, "if you try to explain the Trinity you will lose your mind." This wry warning has been attributed to a variety of sources (including the Church Father Augustine of Hippo, who probably never said anything of the kind), but though the origin is lost, it sums up admirably the dilemma this particular mystery of faith presents for the faithful.

The Doctrine of the Trinity is how Christianity makes sense of Jesus as God. It posits a Triune God—one that encompasses three separate entities, all possessing one single nature (and that one nature is God). Confused yet?

The sixth-century Athanasian Creed puts it this way: "The Father is God, the Son is God, and the Holy Spirit is God, and yet there are not three gods but one God."[1] The Catechism attempts to elaborate: "We do not confess three gods, but one God in three persons, the 'consubstantial Trinity.' The divine persons do not share the one divinity among themselves but each of them is God whole and entire: 'The Father is that which the Son is, the Son that which the Father is, the Father and the Son that which the Holy Spirit is, i.e., by nature one God.'"[2]

Stop here for a moment. Does either of those two official statements offer a satisfactory explanation that helps you understand? Read them over again if necessary. Do these proclamations seem reasonable? Don't feel guilty if they don't satisfy your rationality, even if you're a Christian; it is perfectly okay to want to understand the most basic tenet of your belief system.

When you do, you'll probably come up against more questions.

Does Jesus say anything about the Trinity?

Does the Bible even mention it?

Is the Trinity polytheistic?

Is the Trinity a metaphor?

Did Jesus claim to be God?

If Jesus claims his divinity, does it deny yours? Or mine?

It's tempting to label the Trinity a metaphor, but the Christian Church is emphatic that the three-in-one (or is it one-in-three?) characteristic of this theology is *not* a metaphor; it is a fact. Adherents are to accept it as a basic truth about the nature of God. End of story. The point about polytheism is more delicate: other monotheistic religions of the world have asserted that the

Doctrine of the Trinity violates the most basic tenet of all, that of one single, supreme God.

The accusation stings the Christian consciousness and has caused deep rifts, but it is a fair and reasonable indictment nonetheless. Considered objectively, the doctrine does appear on the surface to be a complication, if not a contradiction, of the very meaning of monotheism. This "complication" is the reason why the doctrine is defended as a mystery of faith, a label that stymies most Christians who might be tempted to delve further into the supposed contradiction. One either blindly accepts the mystery as instructed, or one rejects the mystery as unreasonable and dismisses it as not important.

Back at Santa Maria, once a nun invoked the "mystery of faith" as an answer to one of our queries about doctrine, it was generally not acceptable to continue that particular line of questioning, lest we expose ourselves as Doubting Thomases and bring our faith into question. A good Christian just doesn't challenge a mystery of faith. Questioning one may stir up a feeling of guilt and fear, especially for those who were indoctrinated by nuns. But it's important to remember that the guilt, if you experience any, is just a knee-jerk reaction to your indoctrination; God is not threatened by your examination.

THE JESUS PROBLEM

Nowhere in the Bible is the word *Trinity* or *triune* used. Jesus never used it, nor did any of the authors of the 27 books of the New Testament. So where did the concept come from?

The early Church thinkers faced a challenge: how to handle Jesus, theologically speaking. God, of course, had to remain the central figure of the theology; they couldn't risk the appearance of backsliding to the pagan worship of a pantheon. But they had to decide what to make of this man whom they followed; this man who appeared to know God as none before had known Him. Making Jesus into an additional god would have flown in the face of monotheism, a departure no Jew could accept. (Remember, Jesus and his early followers were Jews.)

In the fourth century, they put it to a vote, as we saw in chapter 6, and declared that Jesus was indeed divine. Even though Jesus described his divinity as something common to all men, Church leaders declared him God in order to obtain the authority they sought. This, in turn, was untenable without some further refining of the concept of God. The very nature of the one true God is overturned, or at the very least revised somewhat, if there is any need to deploy another. It suggests a "division of labor" in the work of God, which implies some limitations to God, which is impossible if God is omnipotent and infinite. So the concept of a triad was formed to explain Jesus' unique divinity, with the Holy Spirit in the third corner: three persons with one nature, extrapolated into the doctrine of the Holy Trinity. It didn't diminish God; it elevated Jesus. The Church could have it both ways.

The Doctrine of the Trinity is so mysterious and complex, so hard to explain, that many fall back on the explanation that it must have come through divine revelation. Revelation is understood as God speaking to man. But this particular dogma was debated and voted upon *man* to man by a body of Church leaders with dissonant views on the matter at the Council of Nicaea in the year 325 CE, using a term that had first been introduced around 180 CE. Though it became part of the Christian vernacular, it had no source in the revelations of a prophet, in the words of Jesus, or anywhere in the Bible, for that matter. *The Trinity was the outcome of mentation, not revelation.* It was fabricated to support the theology *about* Jesus; it does not reflect the theology *of* Jesus.

WHAT DID JESUS SAY?

Jesus discovered at some point that he indeed possessed a divine nature. Maybe, as the nuns taught us, he knew of his divinity from birth, but more likely he discovered it at some point during his human life through his individualized human mind. Jesus certainly seemed to speak of his divinity; he said, "I and the Father are one." But he never claimed to be God. He did claim to be the Son of God, which is not the same thing. He did demonstrate supernatural powers by performing miracles and bending natural laws, and he showed his power over death by his resurrection. But, in each instance, he did so as an example to mankind to show that its nature too was divine. Jesus never intended to separate himself from his human brethren by showing off his divinity. He was proving to us that we were the same as he. He tried to teach his followers that they could do greater things than he had done: "Whoever believes in me will perform the same works I do myself, he will perform even greater works. . . . I shall ask the Father, and he will give you another Advocate to be with you forever, that Spirit of truth whom the world can never receive since it neither sees nor knows him; but you know him, because he is with you, he is in you."[3]

But instead of looking inside to find their own divinity as he instructed them, Jesus' followers instead focused on his divinity, eventually to the point that they made him God. Once they had decided to interpret Jesus' message to mean that he was God, they had to develop a corresponding theology to support it. The principles of monotheism laid down by Abraham, however, couldn't be violated, because Jesus himself referred to the God of Abraham throughout his teaching. So began the development of the theology of the Trinity.

Jesus gave his followers a direction in this by often referring to God as "Abba," or Father, though he was clearly using the term in the sense of God as the Father to all that is, not just his personal dad. He did instruct the Apostles, at the very end of the Gospel of Matthew, to baptize "in the name of the Father and of the Son and of the Holy Spirit."[4] Of course, this doesn't specify, or even intimate, a triune God; Jesus could be saying simply that the singular life force that is God is united with mankind (God's Son) by Spirit. Still, it's not hard to see how the quotation could be made to support the doctrine.

But writing off the Trinity as a bit of fancy footwork on the part of early theologians doesn't deepen our understanding any more than merely accepting it as a "mystery of faith." Let's consider how best to understand this dogma without stopping at either barrier. This is a search for understanding, not an attack or a defense of a specific doctrine, and two different people may come to two different understandings. An open mind is appropriate here.

DO THE MATH

The doctrine of the Trinity is not an easy one to understand. Saint Augustine, who probably did not say it would make you lose your mind, *did* devote hundreds of pages in his masterwork *De Trinitatis* to assessing, unpacking, and attempting to tie up the loose philosophical ends of this counterintuitive concept.

The rational mind has trouble getting past the arithmetic. Three do not in fact add up to one, and one certainly doesn't equal three. One times three equals three, so we can't use the *product* of the three to get one either. When the math doesn't compute, and the "mystery of faith" doesn't hold water, many people either abandon the postulated principle or accept it without any genuine understanding. They may end up adhering lifelessly to the belief system out of duty, bound by guilt, or rejecting it outright.

To get past the math, let's include the entire statement and not just the numbers "three in one." Three of what? One of what? What are these numbers referring to? The *three* is referring to "persons" and the *one* is referring to "nature." The Trinitarian dogma is not saying three persons in one person, or three natures in one nature; it is saying *three persons in one nature*. This points us to the definitions of "nature" and "person" instead of a circular mathematical equation that offers no insight into the possibility of truth behind the doctrine.

A "person" is a being that possesses a certain nature. All beings possess a nature; however, not all beings are persons. Man possesses a human nature and *is* a person; a dog possesses a canine nature, a cat a feline nature, but they are *not* persons. Even inanimate objects possess a nature, such as a tree or a mountain, but they are not persons or even beings. A being possesses a nature; however, a nature does not possess a being or a person in the same way. Being a person answers the question of *who* we are and having a human nature describes *what* we are. You could ask a man *what* he is as well as *who* he is. You could ask about a dog what it is, but not who it is.

Each individual being, whether a person or not, has a nature that it must act in accordance with. Now, the nature may be one it has in common with other beings (or persons), but it possesses it individually. Two cats may be similar and have a feline nature, but each possesses this nature separately. Mankind is made up of individual persons, each with a free will, who share a human nature, yet each possesses his nature within his being, separate from other individuals. So a person is an individual, separate, and stand-alone entity.

"Nature" is that which defines the being. A human (at least a healthy one) does not possess the nature of a dog. A dog does not possess the nature of a fish. The nature of a being determines what that being is. Nature is our modus operandi and person is our identity—the one who does what the nature allows. Our nature is the operating system and our person is the computer, if you'll allow a modern metaphor. We might be able to conceive of a situation where one person or even one being has more than one nature; as an extreme example, think of a person with multiple personalities. But it can seem beyond a stretch to imagine two persons having one nature. The nature seems to be possessed entirely by the person, and it doesn't seem logical that more than one being or more than one person can share a single nature— unless, of course, you are going to apply the logic to God, right? God is infinite and omnipotent, so human limits and possibilities do not apply. So in the doctrine of the Trinity, the Father, the Son, and the Holy Spirit are three distinct *persons* with one single *nature,* and the nature is God.

THE NATURE OF SPIRIT

It's easiest for us to conceptualize the "nature" of Jesus, because we understand him, as human, to be a "person." The nature and personhood of the other two are harder to pin down. If God the Father is a person and the Holy Spirit is also a person, then what do we conclude about God the Father? That He is in some way not purely spirit? Or that some *part* of him is not? And if we understand God as Infinite Spirit, then how is this individual spirit, the Holy Spirit, distinguishable from God? Isn't God *the* Holy Spirit? This is where the doctrine of the Trinity begins to lose traction for me. It seems to impose the kind of separation I have resisted since my days with the nuns—separation that runs counter to the Infinite.

Once you arrive at the understanding that God is pure Spirit—as I described in my own experience in chapter 2—you begin to see that God is infinite as well. Without that personal realization about infinity, I would likely never have gotten to the point of examining the Trinity in this way. That's why I suggested earlier that you contemplate for yourself the idea of infinity as it relates to God. For me, the idea of God as pure, infinite spirit works very well. It allows God to "exist" within the same world I do without too much superstition. It seems more consistent with the teaching of Jesus as well.

Jesus was a personification of God, an individualization of Infinity. This is not a point of contention here. The Infinite Spirit of God permeated Jesus' being, no doubt about it. But Jesus' message was that the Infinite Spirit of God also permeates you and me.

Was Jesus being cryptic and intentionally mysterious about his relationship to God? If he was part of a Divine Trinity, perhaps he had some important reason to reveal only bits and pieces of his nature during his mission on earth. If the Infinite and Omnipotent One wants a nature that embodies three "persons," who's to stop Him? He certainly has the power to do just that. But if that were the case, why wouldn't Jesus teach that more clearly? Why did it take several hundred years and much debate to decipher his message? (I can hear Father Pierre chuckling at me again.)

The aim here is neither to champion the Doctrine of the Trinity nor to debunk it. It is to try to reconcile it with the tenets of monotheism and the teachings of Jesus; to put it in context as a human construct, rather than a revealed truth; and to enable you to ask yourself, "What makes sense to me?" What enhances *your* opportunity to commune with Spirit (which is the real purpose of religion)? Does the belief that God exists within you open a door to better communication with God? Or does the image of a three-in-one Godhead create *more* opportunities for you to commune? Which theology makes God a living and willing co-creator of your life?

NINE

RISE AND FALL

Down Payment on The Deal

I came home from Rome with broadened horizons, a fluent command of Spantalian, and—the main outcome of the year—an agreement in place about the course of my life, signed and sealed by none other than God. In The Deal, I felt that I had accomplished something tangible, and I began to seriously question what value a college degree would add to what I had gained that autumn night in my dorm room. I think I had already made the decision to quit school on some level, but it took a little time for my thought process to catch up to the decision, made somewhere beyond the scope of my rational mind. Certainly, it wasn't practical to quit college, but I began to realize there was a power at work in my life that wasn't completely contained within the realm of the rational. Through the other, inner "knowingness" that I felt more and more I could trust, I knew it was time to move on.

Part of me wanted to leave school and begin the journey immediately, but another part wanted to remain with my friends in college for as long as possible. I very much enjoyed learning and I relished college life. But somehow the events in Rome made school feel trifling; staying in school equated to hiding from the important work I had to do in the real world. I reasoned, presumptuously, that although I was learning in college, I wasn't learning how to make money, which was the must-have commodity I needed to pursue a higher calling. Making money had become my new, true aspiration, and studying theology wasn't teaching me how to do that.

I decided to drop out of Marquette and begin my pursuit of the fortune I was positive awaited me. My older brothers, who had hitherto been a source of guidance, were now engrossed with starting their careers, Bob as an attorney and Tom as a CPA, and my dad was busy establishing a new marriage and a new business, so I was able to slip past those guideposts in my education. I didn't get much encouragement to stay in school, so I dropped out without fanfare.

At about the same time, that strange, blooming "knowingness" unexpectedly showed me the way in another area of life as well. Instead of waiting to get established and get my life on some sort of track, I knew that it was time to ask Lynn to marry me. We had been very good friends in high school and had our first date on graduation night. Throughout our college years and my year in Rome, we were separated by many miles and tested by the normal challenges that come with separation, but our relationship continued to deepen in spite of the distance. There was a tangible positive energy between us that we both felt made us stronger together than we were separately. Though most people saw it as a huge gamble—especially on her part—we were married five months after I got back from Rome. I trusted the voice that told me Lynn was my perfect life partner, and luckily she felt the same way. (Thirty years later, I'm still sure.)

The unfounded confidence I was developing was based on a belief, a *knowing*, that I was *destined* to create a successful life and make a lot of money. I knew I would have to work for it—I still believed in Coach Meyer's lessons about working hard to get what I wanted—but the results were never in doubt. I hadn't yet developed the skill that would later become a hallmark of my career, an ability to analyze situations quickly and incisively; I was moving forward solely on the instructions of that inner voice. By now I had the strong sense I was going to quit working by 40, I just didn't know exactly what path would lead me there, and furthermore, I wasn't all that worried about finding it. I sensed *it* would find *me*. I might not have been able to rationalize or defend my decision, but I believed that some part of me was qualified to make it, and I trusted that part of me, whatever it was.

When a person has no doubt about the outcome of his endeavors, it is amazing how much risk he is willing to take, and I truly had no doubt. I would continue to rely on this kind of belief as my life went on, although I would also develop a personal set of principles for success that had to do with organizing, planning, and goal-setting. Beginning a journey with undiluted conviction frees you to act in bold ways, to accept intuition as guidance, and to trust in something within yet bigger than yourself.

TAKING THE BAIT

Without a college degree, I began to look for work. I soon discovered that the only work I could get, other than labor or factory jobs, was a position in sales. That was fine with me; ever mindful of The Deal, I was attracted to jobs that boasted the most potential for income, and I knew that sales had a big upside.

At first, I was offered entry-level jobs at several stable companies that offered steady income but not grandiose opportunities. But I wasn't looking for safety; I wanted a chance at the big money and I knew I was worth it. Then, in June of 1980, I ran into a very slick recruiter, and although he was vague about the work, I was attracted to his persona and his pitch. Tall and athletic with a deep, resonating voice and a pleasing, confident smile, Jock exuded the easy confidence of wealth. He wore a white button-down shirt with a stylish red silk tie in a half-Windsor knot so tight it bounced on his prominent Adam's apple every time he spoke. The air of formality was tempered by a pair of sunglasses propped casually on the top of his head, laced through his dark, wavy hair. He reminded me of all those executives whose swimming pools I had cleaned the summer before Rome. I felt comfortable conversing with him, and I thought sure I'd made a strong impression on him too, so when he didn't invite me back for a second interview, I called him to ask why.

My call startled him a little, but I could tell he appreciated my initiative. He explained that his company had found little success in recruiting college kids—that the work was aggressive direct sales, often in the inner city, and he was looking for people with a certain amount of street smarts. "You look a little soft," he told me bluntly. I assured him I was hardier than I looked. I told him I'd just returned from a year abroad and meeting people and encountering new cultures didn't intimidate me in the least. He may not have been convinced, but he was impressed.

On the day Jock set for my second interview, I was already scheduled to begin work at another company where I had actually been offered a job. So I turned down that offer—from a retail loan company called Household Finance Corporation that specialized in small consumer loans—and took a chance that I would impress Jock enough to become part of his sales team.

I was sent out for the day to "observe" the position with a rough-looking, tough-talking street kid from Pittsburgh named

Sal, who began the day by lighting up a joint as we drove to his sales territory. The "territory," it turned out, was a residential neighborhood on Chicago's West Side, where he pulled up to the curb in his Mercury Capri and proceeded to hawk kitchenware out of the trunk. After the initial shock wore off, I started helping Sal by corralling people to the back of his car, where he easily and nonchalantly sold about a dozen items, giving most people the impression the merchandise was "hot." This seemed to intensify the urge to buy from him, and at the end of the day, his take from the sales he made was $108.

On the way back to the office in the suburbs, Sal told me that his recommendation to Jock would determine whether I got the job or not. He explained in great detail about the "opportunity" the company was offering to those who passed muster on the streets. He said that this was more than a job, that selling on the street was just a temporary proving ground. The people who proved to be good at selling on the street would be given sales crews to train and then earn money on their sales. The crew leaders who proved to be good supervisors would open branch offices of their own and begin to make the "really big money" that Jock was making.

Sal told me how Jock had been recruited from IBM because he saw a real opportunity to become a millionaire here. Jock, who was a college graduate himself, had been sent to Chicago to open a dozen or more offices; the opportunity to get in "on the ground floor" in Chicago was going to happen fast for those "sharp enough" to get on board. Despite a sneaking sense that I'd been plunked down in the middle of a Dickens novel, I was attracted to the scenario he described. He was using all the right catchphrases to hook a hungry and naive kid like me. Besides, I'd just seen Sal earn over $100 for himself and I knew I could do better.

As we merged onto the Edens Expressway heading north, he asked me very directly, "Do you want the opportunity?"

"Absolutely," I responded without hesitation. I was operating on a gut level, biting on all the bait; big money, opportunity, ground floor, branch manager. I wondered how much The Deal had to do with this unbelievable "opportunity" in front of me so soon back from Rome. I started talking about my travel through Europe and downplaying my college experience, hoping Sal would see me as more streetwise than book-smart. I really felt those experiences had prepared me well to succeed in this type of work; new people, new situations, and different cultures didn't intimidate me. Anyway, The Deal was in play. I was just going to play along.

OLIVER AND FAGIN

Back at the office on Touhy Avenue in Skokie, I found more Dickens: young people, kids really, scurrying about with handfuls of cash, waiting to visit a young lady in a small, windowless office one at a time to turn in Jock's cut from their day of selling. A little pre-scripted drama played out in Jock's office, where he and Sal proceeded to reel me in. Jock played the role of skeptical big shot and Sal convinced him by vowing to take me under his wing. I was offered the "opportunity."

After playing my unwitting part in the scene, I got the job. The next day I showed up ready to have my trunk filled with merchandise to see what I could sell. They explained how most people got two or three more days of training, but because they were swamped with new people, they were "selecting" me to go out alone after just one day of observing because I was one of the "sharper" recruits. Jock loaded me up with 20 assorted pieces of merchandise, including bakeware, luggage, and cheap framed artwork, wished me luck, and gave me his private phone number to call if I needed encouragement or had any problems. I drove about 30 minutes to a town north of the city that I knew pretty well, and with my very first "pitch" I sold 15 of the 20 pieces from my trunk. Since I was starting to view almost everything in my life through the prism of The Deal, I interpreted this as a sign. Selling was the right position for me and I was going to succeed.

For the moment, I was right. I called Jock with the news and he was ebullient in his praise of me. I became his favorite salesperson literally overnight.

Over the next couple of years, I would become something of a company star. After about ten months I had become the youngest manager of a branch, my branch was the fastest to achieve one thousand sales per week, and I was awarded the coveted gold medallion faster than anybody in company history. A manager got an expensive 18-karat limited-edition gold medallion molded in the shape of a figure from Greek mythology when the branch sold over one thousand units a week for four consecutive weeks. We hit that mark the first four weeks we branched off of Jock's operation. My medallion was the Centaur, a half-man-half-beast symbol of strength.

After that, I spawned more new offices faster than anyone before me. I became a fixture on stage at company rallies across the country with a spontaneous speaking style that could ignite large crowds. I was proof that branch managers could recruit college kids, and it changed the culture of the company; soon there were college kids popping up all over the country. My branch sales, and the sales of my offshoot offices, earned Jock hundreds of thousands of dollars. I was Oliver to his Fagin.

I was 22, recently married, driving a brand-new Cadillac Eldorado, living in a big house, wearing expensive clothes, and setting the company ablaze with one sales record after another. I thrived on the recognition and the accolades. I felt like a star, and in the small universe of that company, I was. And as flamboyant as I seemed to the outside world, I kept a secret about the real power behind my success. The Deal I had made in Rome was paving the way for me and I humbly acknowledged it inside. I began to think that maybe I'd reach my destination by the age of 30, not 40.

GROWING PAINS

Sometimes stars flame out, and I did just that. As much drama as I'd created rising to the top of this organization, I made an equally dramatic crash landing at the bottom. It seemed that some of the detail involved in business escaped me and I found myself mired in tax issues and inventory problems. It got worse when I discovered that the inventory problems were the result of employee theft—people were blatantly stealing straight from the warehouse and I was responsible for everything in it. Though I was a star in sales management, I was ill equipped for business management. I trained other new branch managers to get stellar sales results, but I hadn't trained myself in the nuts and bolts of running a business. I was so naive, I thought I was running a "branch" for the company; I failed to realize that they had set everything up in my name so the financial shortfalls in my "branch" were mine alone to remedy.

In spite of the painful outcome, the experience of the rise and fall helped me evolve as a person—to grow in my knowledge of the real world and to advance on my inner spiritual path. It made me stop and take account of myself in a very realistic way. I learned not to cut corners even if those around me were. I learned that I had to become a much better minder of detail. I learned the world is mostly about consequences, that in the end you are accountable for your actions. And I learned the importance of integrity. I was embarrassed and disappointed, but having overcome the disappointment of basketball, I knew I could get past this too.

I learned that I had some innate abilities that would serve me well in the business world—the real business world, not just this marginal street hustle. I realized that I could use the lessons Coach had taught me about leadership, and I found that I enjoyed leading others toward their potential, just as I had when I led one of Coach's camp teams to give their best on the court. I learned that success or failure was a product of the habits I cultivated. I learned some positive habits that I would use for the rest of my business career, and I learned some habits to avoid. I learned how to sell. I cultivated a strong leaning toward entrepreneurism. I developed self-confidence. Most importantly, I began to cobble together a solid set of principles that would produce success throughout my life and that I would later teach to others.

I also learned the valuable lesson of healthy skepticism: that if something seemed to good to be true, it probably was. I learned that some people are willing to exploit others for their own gain. These lessons needed to be learned before I could expect any lasting success and I felt lucky to have learned them while I was young. Since I dropped out of college, I had to get these lessons in the laboratory of life. The financial loss I suffered I viewed as tuition; none of my education to that point had been free, and there was no reason to think it would be free now. But my expectations of succeeding in the long term remained as strong as ever. I still felt the presence I believed to be the source of The Deal.

For the next several years, I kicked around, trying to find my niche. Trying to recapture the glory days, I took another assignment from the company and moved to Canada to open branches there. But my heart wasn't in it any longer. My innocence was gone, and when I could clearly see the cynicism with which the company exploited people's hope, I had a hard time performing at the level everyone had come to expect of me. I lived out of a cheap hotel in Toronto for a few months, far away from my family, until I had finally had my fill of this life. I drove home to Chicago with no money and made it there with about an eighth of a tank of gas to my name. The crash was complete.

DAZED AND CONFUSED

I needed a new plan. Lynn and I had a young child and were expecting another, and I had no job to take care of them. Now began a period of feverishly trying to find my way back to making money again. I worked in the coin-op business for a time, selling vending services to bars and restaurants. I sold insurance for a short time. I sold trucking services for a freight broker. I was marginally successful starting my own discount coupon advertising company.

During this period, I was in a spiritual quagmire, disillusioned and confused. I regretted not getting my degree, but it was too late to go back to school. I was still in my 20s and the one skill I had was in sales, but I was beginning to wonder if I would ever find a "legitimate" sales job. Every one I'd had to that point seemed to be a little dubious, on the fringe, a bit of a hustle. I was good at selling, but my mounting experiences were leading me to believe that sales had an inherently dishonorable bent to it. What could I sell that wasn't a hustle?

I wanted to be proud of my work, proud of what I sold. I wanted desperately to make my mark, to test my skills in a business that I needn't be apologetic about. I wanted to test my principles of success in a more authentic environment. I wanted a job I wouldn't need to explain away.

My spirit was suffering as much as my finances. I attended Mass irregularly and gained nothing from it when I did except a low-level sense of relief that I had fulfilled an obligation. I wasn't feeling good about myself, and my once-budding spiritual life seemed a distant memory. Spiritually, I felt more numb than alive. But I was still mindful of The Deal I had made in Rome and wanted to find another opportunity. I didn't at all feel abandoned by The Deal—I was mad at myself. I knew the past several years were the result of my own bad choices. There was no one else to blame.

I was ashamed and embarrassed for the first time in my life. Shame is a terrible emotion, and I used it to motivate me instead of defeat me. I promised Lynn I was going to find a job in an established industry and become a "hot knife through butter." Though I felt I was ready for something entirely different, I knew I would have to start with a sales position. I was willing to start at the bottom in a conventional industry and work my way up—but where to start?

As I left this period, I was learning important lessons about life—new lessons more pragmatic than pious:

- My actions in the business world had consequences, and they arrived with head-spinning rapidity. The maxim "What goes around comes around" was true—and I couldn't help but notice that the "comes around" part came around faster to me than to others. When I did something well, I got rewarded very quickly. When I goofed, boy, did I pay for it—and fast.

- I was good at selling and good at talking to people. When I spoke before an audience, I wasn't nervous in the least.

- If something seemed too good to be true, it probably was.

- Details in the business world would make you or break you. Mistakes cost money.

- I wanted to find respectable work. What I did to earn money mattered to me.

- Some people exploited others. I didn't want to be one of the people being exploited or doing the exploiting ever again.

TEN

WHO ARE THE CLERGY?

Personnel "Matters"

There are many questions facing the Church as it moves forward into human history, but perhaps none as pressing as the questions about its personnel. The makeup of the priesthood today is one of the most problematic issues for the faithful, especially in an increasingly sophisticated and well-informed marketplace of religious and spiritual "consumers." For many people, the fact that ordination is reserved exclusively for celibate men can create a deep divide—a sense that priests are out of touch with the lives of laypeople, or, worse, that all God's people are not equal in God's eyes.

Division is written into the very language of Church teaching on the priesthood: "No one has the right to receive the sacrament of Holy Orders. Indeed no one claims this office for himself; he is called to it by God. Anyone who thinks he recognizes the signs of God's call to the ordained ministry must humbly submit his desire to the authority of the Church."[1] This authority to allow someone to follow a personal call to the ministry is an authority that the Church gives to itself. Even in the matter of answering one's own call to service, a call from God, the Church places itself squarely between man—especially *woman*—and God. It must step at least a little bit out of the way if it is to survive.

The Church presently takes a very hard line about celibacy and perhaps an even more stringent stand against the possibility of women being ordained. The upper echelon of the Church hierarchy holds firm and resists any pressure from the lay world at large, as if a change in course in any disciplines, doctrines, or practices were beneath it, as if change of this type were unprecedented and impossible. However, the Church has reversed course on issues in the past, mandatory celibacy being one of them. We might have been taught to think of the Church as an immortal, immutable institution whose form is divinely ordained and divinely revealed—but we've seen in earlier chapters that its form is actually a human construct. When the Church views these issues as matter of survival, it will change—surviving is what the Church does.

As we survey the doctrines and practices that dictate who mans the front-line battle stations of the Church, some challenging questions arise.

Does the makeup of the clergy adequately represent the makeup of the faithful?

Does God prefer celibate males to be the exclusive ministers to His human creation?

Did Jesus demand celibacy from his followers or their successors?

Is celibacy scriptural? Is it even doctrinal?

Was Jesus celibate himself?

When and why did celibacy become mandatory?

Were there any female disciples?

The days of holding the faithful in place through brute force and psychospiritual intimidation are waning rapidly. The call for change has not yet reached a level where the Church feels compelled to install new leaders with a more enlightened and progressive attitude toward personnel matters. When the unrest reaches critical mass and the Church realizes that its tight grip on the hearts and minds of humanity is slipping, it will change whatever policies it needs to. There are some within the Church who claim that doctrinal and traditional principles outweigh its instinct to survive, but its foremost principle has been and always will be survival. Of course, the specific questions of celibacy and the ordination of women cry out for change on the merit of the principles themselves; they got it wrong from the start. This change, when it comes, may be more than a matter of survival—not just capitulating to the pressure of modern society, but righting some very old wrongs.

SECOND-CLASS CITIZENS

Any discussion of women's role in the Catholic Church, and to some extent Christianity at large, must begin with the cultural atmosphere in which Christianity was formed. In the first century, women were seen as inferior to men in all ways, with few rights and little public standing. The Church's view of women came directly from the views of society and specifically mirrors Roman law, which can be traced back to Greek philosophy. Not only were women not equal to men, they were repositories of the evil that existed in the manifest natural world.

Roman law granted women no rights, as they were considered men's property, not their equals. A man had the right to treat his wife as he wished and dole out punishment in measures of his own choosing. Women could not own property or inherit it. They could not hold public office, be parties to contracts, or be witnesses in court. Women had the same rights as slaves, criminals, minors, and the mentally deficient. According to Roman law and custom, women simply could not be trusted. The rationale for such harsh treatment was the "weakness" and "stupidity" of the gender.

Aristotle, and to a lesser extent Plato, contributed substantially to this attitude. Plato, who lived four hundred years before Jesus, believed women were a "physical degeneration" of human beings. Aristotle, a student of Plato, took this idea further and taught that women were "defective humans," "infertile males." Even Jewish tradition contributed to this prejudice against women through the Adam and Eve narrative, in which Eve is essentially a by-product of Adam and bears responsibility for colluding with the serpent to bring to an end the bliss of Eden. The fall of man, it seems, was a woman's fault.

The prevailing view in the time when the Christian Church was taking shape was that only a man was fully human, only a man was created in the image of God. Man was believed to be the one responsible for creating new life via his seed. Women were viewed as lesser players in procreation, as they were merely the "field" in which the "seed" was planted; life came from the seed alone, not the medium for the seeds' growth to fruition.

From common law to science, these beliefs have largely been discredited. Gradually, though not yet universally, women have gained political and social stature in the civilized world, but attitudes and religious custom lag behind in many cultures even today. The Catholic Church, like many other Christian denominations, continues to hold firmly to some of the practices, if not the beliefs, that the founders held two thousand years ago. While we could give the founders a pass for deferring to the prevailing views of their time, the modern Church should be allowed no such rationalization. The Church has other positions that offend modern sensibilities, but, to my mind, none as egregious in all its continuing history.

THE ROOTS OF THE DOCTRINE

How does the Catholic Church defend its anachronistic position that only a baptized man can receive the sacrament of ordination (especially in a day and age when women are members of the clergy in many other religions and denominations—think of female rabbis and Episcopal priests)? The strongest argument the Church makes against women being ordained is that the four Gospels report that Jesus chose men to be his disciples. The Twelve Apostles, in turn, did the same when they chose their successors. The Church feels bound by Jesus' choice: "Only a baptized man validly receives sacred ordination. Jesus chose men to form the college of the Twelve Apostles and the Apostles did the same when they chose collaborators to succeed them in their ministry."[2]

Let's look at this more closely. Jesus formed a group of disciples or apostles. A disciple is a follower or student of a teacher, and an apostle is a messenger or representative of a particular position or idea. The word *college* means an organized group of professional people with particular aims, duties, and privileges. But what is often lost in this debate is that the *successors* of these "collaborators"—the ones who actually decided theology and canon—were under the aegis of an already entrenched fraternal organization. The Gospels were chosen many years after Jesus lived, and the texts that suggested Mary Magdalene as a disciple or apostle were suppressed or discarded. Both the Gospel of Thomas and Mary's own testament state clearly that Mary was a trusted disciple, and Peter himself states several times that she was the favored disciple of Jesus.

Even the four approved Gospels of the canon unanimously report that upon his resurrection, Jesus appeared to Mary and other women first of all (one of the few events the four texts all agree on). She in turn was entrusted with the task of spreading the word and telling the other followers of Jesus where to meet the risen Christ. Why Mary? Wouldn't Jesus choose to appear to one who had credibility among the other disciples? Would he use an "outsider" to convey that he had risen? It seems hard to fathom that Mary was merely a coincidental bystander to the most significant event of Jesus' mission. Jesus entrusted her with spreading the "good news" of his resurrection. Isn't sharing the word about the risen Lord exactly what evangelizing is?

The passage I quoted at the beginning of this chapter reads: "No one has the right to receive the sacrament of Holy Orders. . . . He is called to it by God."[3] The very pronoun poses a problem here: it presupposes that God would never call a woman to His service, that God too would view women as inferior in some way to men. This implies that God is a masculine entity or, at the very least, chauvinistic—and a bigoted God is very difficult to comprehend, indeed, difficult for many to worship. A God that is pure Spirit, though, has no gender because it has no body; it has no need to reproduce itself because it is complete and whole in its omnipotence and Infinite Intelligence. God is both male *and* female, and it is hard to believe God prefers one part of human creation over another. The Church is still conforming to cultural conventions that are more than two thousand years old.

JESUS AND WOMEN

When Jesus entrusted Mary with the news of the Resurrection, he was behaving counter to convention but true to his own track record. His treatment of women was indeed unusual for his day and time; *revolutionary* would not be too strong a word. He treated women he encountered during his ministry with respect, dignity, and, most importantly, equality; sometimes his disciples were shocked at the way he interacted with them. He taught women directly, healed them, ate with them, and even had a group of women who traveled with him and his disciples.

Of course Jesus treated Mary, his mother, with the utmost respect, and at times deferred to her, such as when he performed his first miracle at the wedding in Cana, turning water into wine at her request. Mary his mother was with Jesus until the moment of his death, but another Mary, Mary Magdalene, was found near him throughout most of his ministry as well.

Mary Magdalene may well have been a disciple; almost certainly she was the leader of a group of women who traveled with Jesus and his Apostles: "With him went the Twelve, as well as certain women who had been cured of evil spirits and ailments: Mary surnamed the Magdalene, from whom seven demons had gone out, Joanna the wife of Herod's steward Chuza, Susanna and several others who provided for them out of their own resources."[4] These women, probably widows, clearly did more than cook; they paid the bills! This is not the only reference to this group of women who traveled with Jesus. Jesus didn't exactly rail against attitudes toward women in the culture of his day, but his inclusion of them in every aspect of his ministry would certainly have been controversial. The idea of unmarried women traveling with this group of mostly married men would have raised more than a few eyebrows. Jesus clearly trusted these women and ignored society's unenlightened view of them.

Jesus also strayed from the Jewish belief that women should not be taught. In the story of Mary and Martha, Martha invites Jesus to her home for a meal and then appeals to Jesus to get her sister Mary (yes, another Mary) to help her. Mary has been sitting at the feet of Jesus, listening to him preach while Martha prepares the meal. "'Lord, do you not care that my sister is leaving me to do the serving all by myself? Please tell her to help me.' But the Lord answered Martha, 'Martha,' he said, 'you worry and fret about so many things, and yet few are needed, indeed only one. It is Mary who has chosen the better part; it is not to be taken from her.'"[5] Jesus asserts in no uncertain terms the right of Mary to learn from him. He goes further to state that nobody can take that right away. He acknowledges her right to choose and defies anyone to overrule her. Mary was at the foot of Jesus and had the right to remain there. Does this right not extend to other women as well? Couldn't this also mean that a woman has the right to choose a pastoral vocation without anyone denying her the right? Still not sure? Try another passage.

In the Gospel of John, Jesus teaches one of his most important lessons while conversing with a Samaritan woman he meets at a well in the town of Sychar, a place and a people generally avoided by Jews. She was taboo for many reasons—a five-time widow who at that time was "living in sin" and out retrieving water at a time of day not generally acceptable for women to be doing so—but apparently Jesus was not put off.

In his conversation with this woman, he imparts some of his most important ideas about spirituality. On meeting her, he asks her for a drink of water. She is initially surprised that Jesus, a Jew, would even address a Samaritan woman, and even more shocked as he displays knowledge of her life. It is to her, individually, that he delivers the crucial sermon about "living water," explaining that one who drinks the water he gives "will never be thirsty again."

Jesus concludes his message to the Samaritan woman with perhaps one of the single most important parts of his theology: "God is spirit, and those who worship must worship in spirit and truth."[6] Then he confesses to her that he is Christ. The Gospel narrative reports that as his disciples catch up to Jesus, they are surprised to see him speaking to her but not surprised enough to comment: "His disciples returned and were surprised to see him speaking to a woman, though none of them asked, 'What do you want from her?' or, 'Why are you talking to her?'"[7] The woman then proceeds to tell the rest of the town about her encounter with Jesus and many Samaritans beg Jesus to stay with them. He remains there for two days.

Not only does Jesus defy the cultural norm of not speaking to a strange woman of dubious reputation, he becomes the guest of a theretofore unacceptable class of people. The message of equality could not be clearer. Jesus delivers an important lesson to the Samaritan woman, entrusts her to deliver the message to the rest of her people, and then graciously allows them to host him. The Samaritan woman acts in the most literal way as a disciple or minister of Jesus: she delivers the word and the flesh of Jesus to her people. Is this not the action of a minister of Christ?

The Gospel accounts of both John and Matthew also find Jesus relying on the testimony of women to relay news and instructions to his disciples. "Then Jesus said to them [the women] 'Do not be afraid; go and tell my brothers that they must leave for Galilee; they will see me there.'"[8] Jesus is clearly utilizing these women as witnesses to the Resurrection: "Go and find the brothers and tell them: 'I am ascending to my father and your father, to my God and your God.' So Mary of Magdala went and told the disciples that she had seen the Lord and that he had said these things to her."[9]

Isn't this also the work of a minister of Christ—to spread the news of the risen Lord and how to follow him? According to the Church, this work is reserved for men, but evidently not according to Jesus himself.

In the Gospel of Mary and other banned texts, it is suggested that Mary was one of three disciples whom Jesus chose for extra teaching. The others were Thomas and Matthew. This threatened some of the other disciples, particularly Peter, the acknowledged leader of the new movement. In an encounter at a time when the Apostles are scared and confused after the Crucifixion, Peter angrily challenges Mary as she passes along the teaching of Jesus. Mary responds to Peter's scorn by saying: "My brother Peter, what do you think? Do you think I thought this up by myself, in my heart, or that I am lying about the Savior?" Another disciple, Levi, then intervenes and says to Peter: "Peter, you have always been hot-tempered. Now I see you contending against the woman like the adversaries. But if the Savior made her worthy, who are you indeed, to reject her? Surely, the Lord knew her very well. That is why he loved her more than us."[10] Peter's distrust demonstrates that the debate about (and perceived threat of) women leaders in the Church goes back to the very first "pope." How different might history have been had Peter been more open-minded and not so much under the influence of cultural norms?

WOMEN AND THE FUTURE

Continuing to deny women the right to be ordained is the single most perilous position the Church can take for its long-term survival. The arguments against ordaining women are severely out-dated, the rationale for the status quo is increasingly scanty, and the stance against women is more and more indefensible to the modern mentality. It is a position that prompts the world to view the Church as sexist, chauvinistic, and perhaps even misogynistic. Ordaining women is the single most important change the Church must make to survive in the future.

From a practical point of view, the dwindling numbers of priests demand it. The danger of driving women, and the children they raise, away from the Church demands it. Plain, impartial, egalitarian morality demands it. It is inevitable. Any well-run organization would be reconsidering its recruitment policies.

And the argument that the Church cannot depart from Jesus' own recruitment policies contains a major inconsistency. Following the same line of logic, since the men Jesus selected as disciples were all Jewish, only Jewish men should be eligible for the priesthood. So how did the Church adapt its personnel policy to include non-Jewish men as priests? Why were Gentiles acceptable when Jesus clearly chose all Jews? Why did the early leaders take that liberty? Didn't they expand, or change, the scope of Jesus' own selection process to be more inclusive? Would Jesus have objected to the inclusion of women as priests if a church had been his objective in the first place?

The Fathers of the Church took great (and enlightened) initiative in allowing the inclusion of Gentiles; why did they stop at the inclusion of women? Why do they still? Why not adapt to the message of equality that Paul states in Galatians: "You have all clothed yourself in Christ, and there are no more distinctions between Jew and Greek, slave and free, male and female, but all of you are one in Christ Jesus."[11]

A PERSONAL NOTE

I predict this will be the next of the "traditions" to change. If it does not, I believe it will ultimately bring down the Catholic Church as we know it. If the Church is good at anything, it is good at surviving. It may take time, but sooner or later, women will be ordained priests, and the time won't come a moment too soon.

Personally, I find the Church's treatment of women to be archaic and repugnant. To think that Jesus, if he intended to start a church in the first place, would exclude women from ministering to the souls of mankind seems ludicrous, if not unimaginable. The Church views and treats women with the same respect they were given in society over two thousand years ago. One is hard pressed to find one intelligent argument that favors this status quo.

Thomas Aquinas said: "The male sex is more noble than the female, and for this reason Jesus took human nature in the male sex."[12] Aquinas is considered one of the most enlightened theologians in the history of Christianity. Does this statement from such an authority merit defense today? Do the leaders of the Church today actually believe this to be true?

Imagine a group of Church leaders questioning a modern-day Jesus. It would go something like this: "Hey, Jesus, we are contemplating allowing women to minister to the souls of the faithful. We ask your guidance. In your opinion, do you think women have any ability to heal? To teach? To soothe a wounded soul or mend a broken heart? In short, are women as well suited to the priesthood as men?" Jesus would probably walk away laughing, not believing the question to be serious enough to answer. The idea that women can't do the work of priests defies any psychological, spiritual, or practical answer one could attempt to put forth. To believe that women would do anything short of making the Church a more loving institution, a more viable choice in the marketplace of religion, and help it fulfill its true mission seems to verge on the phobic.

Undoubtedly, this is one of the historical hard-line positions bound to crumble in the future. We don't need a crystal ball to see plainly that the Church will not survive forever if it holds to this doctrine. The only obstacle is the hard lines held by men in power. When these men and their hard lines pass the torch to more enlightened and evolutionary leaders, this anachronistic stance toward women will change. Will it be too late? Maybe.

JESUS AND SEX

The celibate priesthood is a fixture on the Catholic landscape today—and a pressing personnel matter that has taken on new importance for Catholics in recent years as some question the relationship between the discipline of celibacy and the hundreds of priests found guilty of sexual impropriety. For this and other reasons, priests and the laity alike are increasingly dissatisfied with the rule of forced celibacy for priests.

Indeed, for more than a thousand years of the Church's existence, celibacy of the clergy was optional. Some clergy members chose this ascetic lifestyle, most likely to emulate Jesus. The apostles, however, were not celibate, nor does Jesus leave any instruction for them to be.

Although it is reasonable and probably accurate to believe Jesus was celibate himself, the Gospels actually state nothing definitive about Jesus' sexuality. Jesus had a completely human experience during his lifetime, so he probably dealt with the urges and impulses most humans do. To say he was asexual or anti-sexual undermines God's creation of mankind as sensuous and sexual beings and probably undermines Jesus' humanity as well. Sexuality is a part of human nature, not some sort of add-on to a "neutral" or androgynous species. Sexuality defines us as men and women. God allows us to co-create with him through the act of sex, so there must be something sacred involved in it.

Jesus most likely celebrated human sexuality without having a need to participate in it; he certainly did not condemn it. In this view, Jesus subordinated his sexuality, which is different from suppressing it; remember, regardless of what other essence or nature we believe Jesus to possess, *he was fully human.* Jesus *channeled* his human appetite for sex, which is the free redirection of that drive toward other values. He sublimated it for his work. There is no record of him asking his followers to do the same.

In a discussion with his disciples about fornication, adultery, and marriage, Jesus explains that some men are able to live a life of celibacy and some are not. "It is not everyone who can accept what I have said, but only those to whom it is granted. There are eunuchs born that way from their mother's womb, there are eunuchs made so by men and there are eunuchs who have made themselves that way for the sake of the kingdom of heaven. Let anyone accept this who can."[13] (It should be noted here that although Jesus used the word *eunuch,* it is generally accepted that he is speaking about celibacy and not actual castration.)

Most of the disciples were married. It is quite likely that these Jewish men held the belief of most Jews at the time that procreation was an important duty of Jewish men. Jesus invites some to "accept" celibacy if they are capable of doing so, but clearly doesn't command it. He shows great insight into human sexuality by acknowledging the obvious difficulty most would have with such a lifestyle. As for Jesus himself, it should be noted that nowhere in the Gospels does Jesus proclaim himself to be such a "eunuch"; he does not proclaim his celibacy. Jesus is assumed to be celibate mostly because, absent any mention of a wife, it is a reasonable conclusion.

A CELIBATE CLERGY

In the Old Testament, single life and childlessness implied a failing or lack of some kind. Abraham is promised by God the "blessing of many descendants"[14]; Jacob's wife, Rachel, says, after she finally gives birth to a son, "God has taken away my shame."[15] This Jewish view of marriage and procreation as a blessing bestowed on mankind was carried over into the early Christian Church. The concept of celibacy was a topic of discussion in the early Church, but it was not adopted as a required discipline for centuries. In 325 CE, the pivotal Council of Nicaea, for example, considered the idea and rejected it. Some early clergy chose to be celibate and follow Jesus' example of sublimation, but it wasn't required of priests for many centuries afterward.

In 1139, at the Second Lateran Council, the Church formally adopted celibacy as a requirement for its clergy. Proponents of the discipline may have argued spiritual reasons for adopting it, but the Church makes no real attempt to hide the economic rationale. If a priest had no responsibility to a family, he could devote all of his time and energy to his vocation, and, even more significant, he would have no motivation to accumulate property or wealth for the benefit of heirs. Church doctrine expressly stipulated that celibate priests avoid the "secularization of Church property." On a priest's death, his assets would remain assets of the Church. The Church would exercise authority and control and sustain economic stability in the process.

THE DOWNSIDE OF THE DISCIPLINE

There is no inherent problem with celibacy in and of itself. Celibacy, as an ascetic lifestyle choice, may free some men and women to perform at a higher level in any number of callings. The problem arises when celibacy is not a chosen path but an enforced practice. A forced discipline loses something compared to one that is entered into freely and happily.

Surveys of Catholic priests show that given the chance to marry, most would. A survey of American priests by FutureChurch finds that 67 percent would marry if given the chance; a survey in Poland suggests that 60 percent would favor the elimination of forced celibacy (noteworthy because Poland is considered one of the most conservative Catholic countries in Europe); the number from a survey in Ireland (where 90 percent of the population is Catholic) is about 60 percent as well, and 30 percent of the priests in the Archdiocese of Milwaukee actually signed their names to a letter to the United States Conference of Catholic Bishops calling for the priesthood to be open to married men.

Fewer and fewer men are entering the priesthood, and their declining numbers must mean something. Is God calling fewer men than he has in the past? Or is the celibate life discouraging men from answering the call? Church officials deny it, but there is no credible evidence that they are right.

It's not much of a stretch to connect the modern phenomenon of sexually abusive priests to the issue of celibacy either. The connection is not as simple as some would make it sound; celibacy does not turn a man into a predator or a pedophile. It's worth considering, though, that the practice of celibacy within a fraternal organization may sometimes attract the wrong type of man in the first place.

Certainly it is too easy to point the finger of blame for "pedophile priests" at celibacy alone; but a systemic problem in the Church seems to have opened the door very wide for people with deficiencies of character. And even those who entered innocently or without deficiency have been left to unworkable devices to deal with such a difficult lifestyle. Priests who went through the seminary many decades ago report an absence of education and training in how to deal with the very real psychological impact of celibacy, and priests today speak of the same.

Many young Catholics point to celibacy as a reason they wouldn't pursue the priesthood. And, perhaps saddest of all, more and more practicing Catholics believe that their parish priests are out of touch with the real problems facing them today. The Catholic laity doesn't totally trust the point of view from which the priests are forced to offer counsel. From a practical standpoint, how is a priest to counsel a man or a woman having marital issues? How much credibility does a priest have when he tells a father of five that birth control is not a viable option? How can a priest comfort a woman who has caught her husband cheating on her? Is it reasonable for a priest to discourage a divorce without any firsthand knowledge of how to make a marriage work? The priest's position can come to seem sanctimonious and irrelevant to a layperson in a life crisis. One regrettable result is that the layperson may become more suspicious of celibacy than appreciative of the sacrifice the priest is making.

Time has a way of changing everything in the manifest world; the only entity beyond change is the Infinite One. As stubborn as the Church seems to be, we shouldn't be fooled into thinking it is immortal; it is not. Throughout history, the Church has done what it needs to in order to ensure that it moves with mankind into the future.

The Roman Church has done reprehensible and detestable things throughout its history, but survival has always been the end that justifies any violent or unjust means. Now that the days of forcing itself upon mankind through violence and intimidation are over, the Church will have to adapt to whatever challenges the future may bring. (Or it won't.) Considering its track record of wiping out opposition from within (the Inquisition) or without (the Crusades) in the name of survival, ordaining women or allowing priests to once again marry seems like a minor concession.

If the Church will not evolve along with the rest of humanity, then it will find its rightful place on the proverbial trash heap of history and mankind will find its own way forward—a brotherhood (and sisterhood) of man (and woman) responding together to the primal divine call, the Ascending Urge of the human race.

ELEVEN

THE DEAL DELIVERS

God's End of the Bargain

In March of 1987, I accepted a position at a daily newspaper in Waukegan, Illinois, selling ad space for $300 a week. This was considerably less than I had been earning before, but at least I had kept my vow to find a more conventional industry in which to ply my skills.

I was given a territory well out of the main trading area of the newspaper in a neck of the woods where the company hoped to make inroads. The salesperson before me had had a good rapport with the advertisers in the area but reported there was no growth potential because the territory was too far from our core base of readers. They were testing my ability, and I was enthused to prove I could sell despite the low historical performance of the territory. I was very grateful for the opportunity. And within just a few days, I knew this was the business I would stay in for the rest of my career.

Again, I couldn't elucidate this knowingness, but it was palpable. Like the signal I got on my very first day of selling junk, which I took as a sign that selling was the right position for me right then, I got strong signals that I was going to find great success here at the Waukegan *News Sun.* I understood that my past sales jobs were part of my evolution in the business world, and despite the upheaval they'd created, they would help me immensely now.

I found selling advertising for a daily newspaper refreshing; the credibility of selling a more mainstream product, one I didn't need to explain or rationalize, was good for my self-image. I was excited and proud to be working in the "Fourth Estate," as the print media likes to refer to itself. From the very beginning, I had a romantic notion that I was doing something more important than just peddling stuff. I was selling a product that directly supported an institution that was protected in the Constitution. Newspapers played an important part in our nation's history, and without advertising, there is no newspaper. This was work I could be proud to do. Besides, I quickly found I liked it very much.

I liked working with small merchants and corporate managers alike to help them sell more of whatever they were selling to the public, be it service or product. I might spend time working with a mom-and-pop florist on an advertising program to sell more floral services, for example, and in the process learn a great deal about marketing flowers. Then I might find myself with a small group of executives at an upscale marina, devising plans to sell more $50,000 boats, and learn about marketing big toys. I caught on quickly about how to use demographic and readership statistics to sell advertising. For example, I would take income statistics for a town or ZIP code and then combine them with our circulation and distribution in the same area to convince the marina that our readers could afford to purchase their boats. Or I'd use statistics on age and employment to show a child-care center where all the working moms lived; then if we had readership in those areas, the sale was easy. And because I sincerely believed in what I was selling, I found it easy to take business from competitors.

As I got entrenched in my new, gratifying, self-respecting job, life began to stabilize for me. I started going to Mass regularly and found great comfort once again in the familiar sights, smells, and sounds of Catholicism. The cadence of the Mass had remained the same since my days as an altar boy, and rising and sitting and kneeling in unison with several hundred other Catholics seemed to offer an important continuity to my life—a palpable link to my childhood. It felt good to be "back home" again. And as the ritual of attending Mass once again became a cornerstone of my weekly routine, I spontaneously began a habit of gratitude. Things began to go so well for me that I was reluctant to petition for anything in prayer, so instead I prayed with thanksgiving for all that had happened the previous week.

Even more significantly, this was the first time I was really connecting or communing since I'd attended daily Mass in Rome. Mass for me had always been comforting in its communal rituals, not in any personal connection I was making with the Divine. The prayers of the Mass and its sacramental element, while satisfying a sense of duty, were simply too ritualistic to touch me in any personal way. The gratitude I was beginning to experience now felt organic and natural—and new—while the familiarity of Mass gave me comfort and continuity. I had learned to *expect* guidance and foresight, so I didn't ask for help; I just remembered to offer thanks for the continuous stream of good fortune and clear vision that was coming my way.

THE CORNER OFFICE

A newspaper ad rep was traditionally a service-oriented position, one that called for the newspaper rep to act much like a courier who transferred ad materials to the production department, then brought proofs to the advertiser to inspect prior to publication and delivered tear sheets of the ad upon publication. There was little actual "selling" going on. A person like me, more oriented toward direct sales, was an anomaly in newspapering at the time. This distinction would prove to loom large in my career, and learning to hustle was already beginning to pay off in big ways. I knew The Deal was being executed as events in my newspaper career launched me to higher plateaus than I had ever imagined.

I had gotten into the habit of setting daily, weekly, and monthly goals for myself, and I hit each target I aimed at in rapid succession. Using my proven work habits and principles, I was able to call on approximately ten times as many advertisers as my counterparts. The rest of the sales staff typically left the office at about 10:30 a.m. after drinking coffee and reading the paper, then drove around, picked up ads from three or four regular advertisers, delivered tear sheets, met up with each other for lunch, and returned to the office around 2:00 to get their ads processed so they could leave precisely at 5:00. I was just returning to the office about that time after calling on 20 to 30 advertisers; I'd be getting off the elevator as the rest of the staff was getting on. I would stay until 6:30 or 7:00 to get my ads processed and plan the next day. During my first month, I more than tripled the sales from the previous year, and I would keep this up for the duration of my time on the street.

I advanced from ad rep to advertising director in six months. Life was good and getting better. I had a responsible job at a reputable daily newspaper and I was beginning to contribute at a high level. I was given the northeast corner office on the fifth floor of our six-story glass-and-metal building on a bluff overlooking Lake Michigan. I was in that office before dawn every morning to greet the sun as it yawned itself awake rising over the water, warming me through the glass as I planned and plotted my course. I used this quiet time to begin to devise systems and structures that would allow, or induce, the sales staff to sell more and service less. Using the leadership principles and management strategies I was developing, I restructured sales territories, compensation plans, and processing systems to post substantial departmental sales gains. My income was rising sharply now that I had a good base salary and a lucrative incentive plan based on revenue growth.

I was pleased with the direction of my life and proud of my success, if not altogether content. I was making all the right moves and it felt like there was something out in front of me clearing the way for me, too. Everything I tried succeeded hugely. And the more success I had as an ad director, the more confidence I began to have in myself and the more faith my superiors placed in me. I was continually met with open doors and open arms. With Coach Meyer's mantra in my heart, *hard work pays off,* I continued to work very hard and put in long hours, but in truth, it all felt easy—natural, like I was born to be a newspaperman. Newspapering felt more like a game than work, and I loved to play the game. Rarely were my ideas or initiatives rejected.

The publisher I worked for, Mr. Pfeil, actually reminded me of Coach Meyer a little, and he claimed a similar role as a mentor. He was an elderly man who had come out of retirement to run the *News Sun* as an act of friendship to the owner of the newspaper group. Soon after I became the ad director, he put me on his inner-circle management team. Now I was attending twice-weekly meetings with the other department heads, seasoned newspaper pros. We met in the dark-paneled boardroom next to Mr. Pfeil's office on the sixth floor every Tuesday and Thursday at 8:00 a.m. My newspaper learning curve took a very sharp upward turn at these round-table strategy sessions as I absorbed the knowledge of some very experienced executives about all the aspects of newspaper management.

I became the youngest member of a group of managers who went to lunch together every day, and there, too, I learned just by listening. We played poker once a month, went to ball games, attended charity events, and were involved in all the happenings in town, from judging beauty pageants to riding in parades. I felt privileged and challenged to be in the company of this group. Little did I know life was actually training *me* to be a publisher some day not far off.

THE LONE WOLF

In the late '80s, the newspaper business was severely challenged by increased competition, rising costs, and diminishing revenues (not to mention the service mentality of sales departments). While many other dailies were suffering through slumps, our paper was boasting 20-percent-plus advertising increases. The increase in revenue let us make bold moves in other areas of operation.

In the spring of 1990, I was invited to write an article for a trade journal about my techniques and then to speak at the state press association convention to discuss them with other ad directors and marketing executives. The rest of Illinois wanted to know what was happening up in Waukegan. I gave a talk about some of the basic strategies we were implementing in our ad department, speaking mostly in general terms about the transformation we had made from a service-oriented staff to a proactive sales organization. I presented to the group the management principles and techniques I was using to grab a larger market share.

As I mingled with the attendees afterward, a seed of an idea was planted when a marketing director from Moline asked if I would come and work with him and his staff to help implement some of my techniques for running an ad department. I brushed this off as cocktail-party banter, but he kept insisting that I give him a price for my services. He was certain his boss would pay "serious money" to get my program installed in their newspaper. He pointed out that they were about two hundred miles away so they posed no competitive threat to the *News Sun*. When he told me that the owners of his paper also owned five or six others, and that the owner believed in hiring outside consultants, he got me to think about it seriously. Meanwhile, I began to conduct regional educational workshops for the Illinois Press Association and give keynote speeches for the Inland Press Association. These gave me a chance to test my management concepts further in public and to explore the idea of going out on my own as well.

Several months later I was off to start my own consulting business. I was 31 and by now I had a mortgage and three kids, but I quit a six-figure job to venture out on my own as a consultant—a lone wolf, as one-man consulting firms are known. My plan was to conduct workshops around the country to establish my name while I tried to build the consulting part of the business. I figured it would take several years to establish enough of a client base. Meanwhile, the workshops alone tripled my income from the position I had had at the newspaper.

I was right about the workshops building a consulting practice, but I was wrong about how long it would take. Instead of two or three years, it took about four months. After that, I quit doing workshops because my dance card was full with consulting engagements. Each workshop led to at least one consulting contract and almost every consulting contract led to another. Some of my original clients were part of newspaper groups, and when the results started to come in I was engaged to work at the other papers in the group. I had clients from Boston to San Francisco, and money began rolling in at a surprising rate. Soon I was completely booked and had to draw a line on how many clients I could adequately serve at one time.

My clients were small to medium-sized dailies, some in hotly contested suburban markets, others in sleepy rural markets with little competition. Both of these scenarios were well suited to my expertise. The suburban dailies were familiar because I had cut my newspaper teeth competing in Chicago suburbs, one of the few markets that had two major metros: the *Chicago Tribune* and the *Chicago Sun-Times* hotly competed for the same readers and advertisers as the *News Sun,* and that prepared me to help my clients in competitive markets. My other clients, the isolated, sleepy little dailies, were so used to not having competition that they had become complacent, so they were prime candidates for significant growth as well. After billing for my initial retainer, I was paid on the revenue growth, so the consulting contracts were relatively easy to sell (if they didn't grow, they didn't pay) and could be very lucrative depending on the revenue base I had to work with. Many of my clients boasted seven-figure increases during the first year I worked with them, and I collected a percentage of that increase. I was starting to make real money.

During this period, I was traveling a great deal, spending long stretches of time alone. I used the solitude to take account of the awesome power operating in my life. I kept thinking of The Deal made just ten years before. I recognized a serendipity and synchronicity manifesting in my life now that I would come to describe as providence, and of course, the providence was a direct result of The Deal. I was fully aware of the limits of my ability, because I had experienced failure early, but in what I could accomplish in business, I felt limitless. I began noticing that whatever I began to seriously think about would manifest itself in my life. Driving along in silence from one job to the next, I would ponder for hours whether I was actually doing the thinking or whether my life was being "thought" by something greater than me. I didn't know if I had this much capacity to achieve or if I was just along for the ride. The money was nice, but I never got too hung up on it. I still believed that I was supposed to do more than just make a lot of money. I understood money to be a tool I needed to accomplish that something more.

THE ROAD TO SPIRIT

There was one thing about this period that I became aware of only later. I think I was attributing the streak of positive occurrences in my life to my relationship with the Church, thinking that somehow my good fortune and the results manifesting in my life were due to my being a "good Catholic." I wasn't giving much thought to the idea that on that spiritually charged evening in Rome, The Deal had been made with a much higher power than the Church. I was still *mentally* connecting God to the Church, even though *spiritually* I should have known better. This idea that the Church was the mediator, the intercessor between me and the Infinite Power at play in my life, was so dominant to my way of thinking, so central to my indoctrination, that I completely overlooked the reality of what had happened that night. It would take several more years to understand the real essence of The Deal. Right now, I didn't fully comprehend what was happening, I was just mindful of being grateful for it.

My career so far had been a series of micro-sprints toward one objective after another; every time I accomplished a goal, I set a new one. My mind was occupied by my worldly objectives and my energy was consumed completely each day. Still, every Sunday I made some time to attend Mass and say thanks.

Going to church was a habit—I attended Mass because I believed I was supposed to—but the service was primarily a weekly period of reflection for me. I began to tune out the liturgy and just sit there and count my blessings, always thankful, never asking for anything material in my life. I was reluctant to ask because my needs were being so well tended to by life's opportunities that I didn't want to limit my experience by specific requests—I understood providence was in play. It seemed the more I gave thanks, the more I received.

At the same time, my view of life became more and more transcendental as I began to have more solitude. As I became less and less engaged in the Mass, I somehow became more and more engaged with Spirit. Occasionally I even began to question the necessity of the institutional intermediary I was employing in my relationship to the entity I had been trained to call God. Because of the travel involved in my consulting work, I was spending more time alone than I had since I left Rome. Sometimes, during the hours on the road or in the air, I would be overcome by a rush of raw excitement. I felt truly alive and vital and exhilarated by my life. At first I thought it was excessive sentimentality, and it made me a little uncomfortable. But as it began to happen regularly, and as I reflected on it, I began to realize how spiritual a being I really was, how spiritual we all have the potential to be.

The state I occasionally found myself in that left me feeling a little embarrassed was somewhere beyond my ability to rationally understand. Looking back on it now, though, it explains why I was successful: I was extremely happy to be alive. To be in that state of joy is the most attractive a person can be to the world, and I was attracting all kinds of positive results. Many clients reported that they saw improved morale and better results just by having me on the premises. They told me how the energy level in the entire operation was affected for days after I left. Without understanding *how* this was happening, I *knew* it was true.

It wasn't emotion that was gripping me, it was a growing metaphysical realization—a spiritual awareness similar to, though still not as dramatic as, the experience in Rome. I was beginning to feel the presence of "God" more in my car or on an airplane or in a hotel room than I did in church. When my mind tired from the day's action, I inadvertently opened a channel to Spirit, and what came through was guidance with total certainty of my direction. I can remember driving the famously flat, straight roads of Indiana with my windows and top down, basking in the sun and wind, losing all awareness of conscious thinking. Details about clients, employees, or directions to my next destination disappeared from my mind while some other kind of awareness took over. For someone who was so detail-oriented within the walls of a newspaper plant, it was amazing how many times I ran out of gas, got a speeding ticket when I was in no particular hurry, or forgot to stop and eat. I was literally *feeling* the Spirit in charge of my life, not sentimentally but with an almost physical sensation of presence, like that long-ago trip to Texas when I had God in the shotgun seat.

The Deal was indeed being played out and I suspected the time was coming for me to follow through on my end. I knew I was going to be given a responsibility to communicate ideas buried deep in the memory of what had happened in Rome all those years before. The closer I got to age 40, the more awed I became at the prospect. I still didn't exactly know what form it would take. I assumed I would become an apologist for the Catholic Church. I mean, what else would it be? What else did I know?

THE BIG MOVE

After four years of growing my consulting business, I found another opportunity on my path and I knew for certain this was the clincher. This would be the big score that would give me the chance to quit working, at least in the realm where I had been working, and place the onus on me to hold up my end of The Deal. I was almost 36.

Around Thanksgiving 1994, acting on an impulse that took me by surprise but seemed inevitable at the same time, I made an overture to a client to buy one of their daily newspapers that was failing in its suburban market. John, the gruff, chain-smoking president of the company laughed at me for even suggesting it. From my position as consultant to several of the newspapers in this group, I knew how poorly it was performing and how it was dragging on the profitability of the company at large. John informed me that 20-some other newspaper companies had looked at the operation and nobody had even made an offer. The rumor mill reported that the paper had already been declared dead; there was no reviving it. But John reluctantly reported my overture to the family who owned the company, and when he called me back within half an hour telling me they wanted to meet with me, I was sure we would strike a deal.

The knowingness I had been experiencing now for several years told me that I was the one to turn the paper around. The rational part of my brain concluded I had nothing to lose by trying, while something deeper and bigger than my brain "knew" I would succeed. My life had trained me to trust this knowingness and I pushed persistently for this transaction. I wouldn't take no for an answer. By Christmas, John's cynicism notwithstanding, we had a deal. I took over the *Olathe Daily News* in suburban Kansas City in February of 1995.

Undaunted by the poor prospects, I summoned new energy to throw at this project, more energy than ever before. My faith in the ultimate outcome never wavered for one minute. Of course, there were sleepless nights when my mind worried about how to make it all work, but my spirit rested in the knowingness that I had been given a great opportunity to make good on my end of The Deal. I knew I would succeed.

Life as a newspaper publisher was heady and exciting. My arrival in Olathe coincided with a sort of renaissance there, and as we got involved more in local affairs, the town showed great support for our enterprise. And the uncanny synchronicity continued. I would meet people who seemed to be put in my path just to help me. I would find books that filled a particular void in knowledge that I needed to fill at just the right time. Employees would come on board with the exact skill sets we needed.

I remained thankful, in the mode of gratitude for all that was transpiring in my life and in my business. I still felt I didn't need to bother asking for anything—all I needed was being delivered, it seemed, magically and right on time. I wasn't tempted in the least to "help" the providence so obviously working in my life; I worked very hard myself and simply trusted the communication that kept coming to me through my inner knowing. It helped tremendously that my family had adapted nicely and was thriving in our new home.

Spiritually, I was missing the solitude of those times on the road visiting my clients, but the work in Olathe was challenging and rewarding. I woke up every morning excited to go to work. I had the incredible feeling of doing with my life exactly what I believed I was intended to do. Running a newspaper came naturally and intuitively, and I was well prepared, thanks to my experience in Waukegan working for an old master publisher and then traveling the country to get involved in nearly every conceivable situation that a newspaper could find itself in.

Of course, it wasn't all smooth sailing. Our first 18 months were filled with misfires and setbacks. We started a new weekly publication in another town that was met with critical acclaim and great reader response, but that town was just beginning to develop economically, so advertising dollars were still off in the future. We took the market by storm but didn't turn a profit for some time. To boost revenue, we ventured into selling commercial printing—essentially, printing newspapers and other periodicals for publishers who didn't own their own presses—but soon found we were not staffed with enough well-trained pressmen or supervisors to handle the extra work. In one desperate afternoon, I and the entire management team—general manager, circulation director, ad director, and business manager—went chasing around rural grocery stores, hand-inserting ten thousand grocery fliers into papers for our largest new customer because our mailroom had forgotten to insert them before they were shipped. We were aggressively trying to build the business, but we were losing money in just about every way you could lose it. Expenses? Too high. Revenue? Too low. Employees? Too many. Seasoned managers? Not enough.

OPEN THE BOOKS

After almost a year and a half of working very hard to get the *Daily News* turned around, I began to see that to keep from going belly up, we needed more radical change. We had started a couple of new publications, mostly to justify the number of employees we had. We had won awards for quality in several areas. But we weren't really making any profit. I was manipulating cash flows to keep us afloat and I was rapidly running out of money from the nest egg my consulting practice had built. I was tempted to follow the well-worn path of laying off workers in order to meet our budget constraints, but that seemed the easy way out and, to me, it never seemed the correct way. You build a company with good people, and we had some pretty good people; getting rid of them seemed a step in the wrong direction.

During the very early days in Olathe, I was reluctant to tell my staff the hard truths about our vulnerability, but now it began to wear on my conscience. Though there was good news—we were making progress on several fronts—to focus only on the positives and not be frank about the negatives seemed dishonest, even disrespectful. And furthermore, if people only saw part of the problem, how could they offer anything to me but part of the solution? I believed my strongest asset as a manager was to mobilize people toward common objectives, to motivate them through a sense of mutual respect and loyalty. I expected the whole truth from my team, and in return, I concluded, I needed to tell them the complete, unadulterated truth about the paper's situation without any corporate-speak or spin.

This ran counter to all my training in the corporate world, where we were taught never to share bad news with our staffs. We weren't supposed to distract them from their individual work by showing them the big picture. Further, we were told, employees didn't really care about the company; they only cared about collecting their paychecks. If they knew we were vulnerable, they would begin to look for work elsewhere. That had never felt to me like the right way to manage people, and I'd been scolded on several occasions at the *News Sun* for sharing too much information with my staff. Now that I was responsible for the company, with nobody up the chain to answer to, I could reject this attitude if I really wanted to. I could test my inclination to trust my people. The question was, did I have the guts to do it?

On a chilly, wet, and gloomy April morning at the hotel, I decided to come clean. I assembled the entire workforce for a Saturday-morning meeting at the local Holiday Inn. I instructed members of my management team to set up a table outside the meeting room and have outside employment counselors sitting there ready to help any employees who decided it was time to move on. I fully expected that when the truth was told, some would opt out for safer employment prospects. But the whole team argued against this, and they finally convinced me. They would prove to be right.

For three hours that morning, I showed charts, analyzed spreadsheets, and told stories about turnarounds from my consulting days. And my employees listened. I was amazed that not only were they all interested in the business side of newspapering, they actually understood it. I told them we were improving but still at risk. I explained how newsprint costs, for example, had increased 65 percent since the day I took over. I reminded them that the managers were committed to not laying off workers—that instead we were creating more work via new publications and new entrepreneurial ventures, but some of those were not yet profitable. I told them we had a great team assembled but there was still a very real possibility we wouldn't make it.

After the initial shock, I sensed a change in the room that I could never have anticipated. My management team was right, nobody wanted to quit. Instead, I saw the group light up with something that could only be described as newfound dedication. They appreciated the respect I was showing them by telling them the truth, and I felt their trust in return. When I opened the floor for discussion, they told me they knew things weren't good but felt helpless to do anything about it because they didn't understand where we were hurting. They started to come up with ideas and wanted to form committees to break down all the information. There was not one person in the room who wanted to abandon what we had started together. When we came out of the window-less meeting room, the gloom of the morning had given way to a gloriously sunny spring afternoon. We left the Holiday Inn as a new company. And we all knew it.

Our people had inspired the management team and me to work out a system of sharing results so they could know where we stood as we moved forward from that day. We tried to devise a system of scorekeeping, but we were frustrated at first and got bogged down in a myriad of detail that seemed to distract instead of direct our collective energy toward meaningful reporting. The numbers were thick, and the density of the information began to make people's eyes glaze over instead of sharpening our focus as we'd intended.

Since I was about 23 years old I'd been making monthly visits to the bookstore. (I think I was trying to compensate for leaving my college degree behind.) Many visits had a goal—I was going to buy a book or books I had heard about. But often I simply went looking for more knowledge about business or management, anything to sharpen my skill or increase my insight, and rarely was I disappointed. The synchronicity at work in my life never seemed to elude me; I always came home with something of value to the path I was on, and often an answer to a specific situation I found myself in. On such a visit, shortly after this spring meeting when I was struggling with the promise I had made to find a meaningful way to share results, a book practically jumped off the shelf at me. It was called *The Power of Open-Book Management.* Synchronicity strikes again! Someone else had already done what we were trying to do, and this book gave us the very blueprint we were looking for.

A few days later, on the phone with my good friend and benefits consultant Marnie, I explained to her my enthusiasm for this new book I had found. "Wait a minute," she said. "Who wrote that book?" When I told her the author's name, she shrieked, "She's one of my good friends! Would you like to have lunch with her?" I was delighted to learn the author was from Kansas City, but I was becoming so accustomed to the synchronicity in my life that I wasn't really shocked. When I met the author, the late Jill Carpenter, she was charmed by our company's story and agreed to work with us on an unusual compensation plan: she trusted us to us pay her as we accomplished the turnaround, which we did in an astoundingly short time.

We went from losing about $25,000 a month to an 18-percent average monthly profit in about eight weeks. Once Jill helped us post our financial results in real time, we turned our business into a game. The object of the game began as simply "saving each other's jobs" and rapidly progressed to specific profit-margin targets and a bonus system tied to every single line on the P&L, which, in turn, found each and every employee eligible for bonus payouts. The peer accountability this brought to the workplace made managing much less about putting out fires and more about seizing growth opportunities. Soon we were dominating the contest circuit with awards for quality, pounding our competitors, and making double the margin most daily newspapers were earning at the time. My management principles and tools were evolving once again.

I saw all this, as you might guess, as a truly transformational and even transcendental event. When the tension that naturally arises in a company with five different departments with naturally opposing interests is replaced with a spirit of cooperation and genuine concern for each other (as well as financial incentive), miracles happen. The stories are too numerous to tell here: every day, most days more than once, an employee would come up with a cost-saving or revenue-producing idea that really mattered. Interdepartmental teams and committees spontaneously sprouted, creating harmony where conflict had reigned, and the harmony always impacted the bottom line. A palpable new spirit permeated the workforce and the management team from that day at the Holiday Inn—an *esprit de corps*—and this spiritual addition to our workforce would prove to be the missing link in our success. We all felt it pulsing through our twenty-thousand-square-foot hive of business enlightenment, and we knew we had tapped into something very special. I used to brag that "pound for pound" we had the toughest, most proactive daily newspaper staff in the U.S.

CASHING IN

A couple of years after the dramatic turnaround at the *Daily News,* things changed in the newspaper business. When I had bought the company, newspapers were not viewed as very attractive properties, so I'd been able to negotiate a pretty low price. Then in 1999 papers became hot properties again and began to sell for record multiples (probably for the last time; today, newspapers are dying off at an alarming rate and must morph into something new in order to survive). A newly formed newspaper group headquartered in Texas came to town with a large bankroll from Wall Street and began looking for properties to "roll up," that is, buy. They immediately paid a premium price for a competitor of ours, a weekly newspaper that had been in town for many years. The owner of that group of weeklies was a second-generation operator who had my respect and had become a friend.

Soon after buying out my friend and competitor, the Texas group came snooping around our paper and I began talks with them about selling the *Daily News*. Negotiations fell apart one evening when the president of this new company got drunk at dinner and came down with a severe case of loose lips. He began to talk about his former company, which happened to own the *Kansas City Star,* the major metro newspaper in K.C.; he poked fun at the publisher of the *Star,* who, in my opinion, was one of the single classiest publishers in America, and he giggled about my friend, the publisher/owner of the weekly he had just bought. And he didn't limit his disparaging remarks to local publishers who were not present—he made a remark about me being a small-town operator, a "hick" who'd gotten his break by inheriting the newspaper from his family. He wasn't just drunk, he was ill prepared for this meeting, apparently confusing me with some other owner they were trying to buy out. He hadn't done his homework on me, that's for sure—I'd never inherited a dime, let alone the *Daily News*—and his "hick" remark insulted me. He didn't know I was from Chicago, and one thing you should never do is call a Chicagoan a hick.

He kept drinking throughout dinner, and I began to conclude this wasn't a company I could trust, not because he was drinking but because of the character he was revealing when his inhibitions went down. I didn't trust them to complete the transaction with honor, and I especially didn't trust them to treat my loyal employees with dignity after they took over. One skill I retained from my days hustling kitchenware on the streets of Chicago was how not to be intimidated by a bully. I told this guy I didn't think it was wise for me to do business with people who were drunk, and I left before the main course was over.

The next morning, one of his finance people from Wall Street who'd been at the dinner called, apologized profusely for the behavior of the CEO, and asked me to meet them in a room they had rented at the airport. The CEO was sheepish and seemed to want to forget his boorish behavior. I played along, but I felt sure I would never sell the *Daily News* to such an obnoxious and treacherous man. I had contempt for him mostly because of the things he had said about my friend and former competitor, whose operation he had just purchased. After trying to smooth over my feelings from the night before by explaining how they wanted to retain me to run the entire K.C. operation, my small group of papers as well as the ones they'd just purchased, they invited my friend into the room and they proceeded to ambush me. The conversation quickly shifted to the working relationship they wanted to create between us, and it was immediately obvious they had presented us with two completely opposite scenarios. The CEO's duplicity was on full display, and I suspected he would not honor either one. I was thoroughly disgusted by this slickster and my instinct told me this would be the last time I would ever see him again. My instinct was right. I did, however, keep the lines of communication open to the New York financial people until I negotiated a deal with another party to buy my paper. (I kept checking to see if they'd replaced the drunk with a more honorable newspaperman.)

Everything was in perfect alignment and the time to sell the paper was now. Suburban dailies were the hottest of all the hot newspaper properties and mine was performing exceptionally well. I could fetch a high price and I had a sense the window of this opportunity would not stay open too very long. Furthermore, I was almost 40, and the timing of the events was not lost on me.

Over the next year, many variables had to synchronize in order for me to sell the operation to the company I preferred. A large national newspaper group, Knight-Ridder, had owned the *Star* for several years, and when they bought that paper it came with a judgment in place since 1957 that prohibited them from buying or owning any other media operations in the metro area. After delicate negotiations (which involved the government), the consent decree was lifted in order for Knight-Ridder to purchase my company. They were considered one of the most employee-friendly newspaper companies in the country, so my people would be in good hands; they were willing to pay me in cash, which meant no stock options from a fledgling company run by a drunk; and they didn't feign interest in retaining me. They gave me the money, I gave them the keys, and it was a done deal.

Speaking of deals, I was 13 months past my 40th birthday on the day we closed. The Deal was real, and I knew that it was now my turn to live up to it. I still had no clear idea what exactly I would be living up to, but as I left this part of my life behind, I was sure life was just beginning.

What I knew at this juncture was:

- I had a talent and a love for bringing groups of people together to achieve common goals. I'd proven this in my consulting practice and at my newspaper.

- When people connect to something bigger than themselves, they accomplish more than they think they can. And the bigger the goal, the more likely they are to achieve it.

- Giving thanks for what you have gets you more than asking for things that you don't have. The more you appreciate the people, events, and things in your life already, the more you receive.

- All achievement starts as an idea. You manifest exactly what you think you will.

- I could find an element of spirituality in achieving goals in the physical plane.

- The Deal was real.

TWELVE

WHO IS JESUS?

Christ Consciousness
and the Kingdom Within

As a small child I would sit by the flocked Christmas tree in our living room and gaze into the Nativity scene for hours, imagining the cold and wintry night Jesus was born, how the three wise men brought him gifts, and that the infant in the manger knew just why they traveled so far to worship him. At Santa Maria, we were taught that Jesus, even as a newborn, understood who he was and what his purpose would be.

For many years I had no cause to question that simple understanding of Jesus, his life, and his message. Like many, I assumed he was the one who started the Church and generated everything related to it, including the doctrine. So when I began to question Catholicism, I naturally began wanting to reexamine my understanding of this historical and biblical figure. Jesus was always a compelling character in the story of Christianity for me. Even when I finally admitted I had some conflict with dogma, I never felt any conflict with Jesus. What was it that allowed me to keep the two separate in my mind and heart?

Throughout this book we have examined the intersection

between what Jesus said to his followers and what the Church instructs its adherents to believe, and we've seen that they don't always match up. Even when I found myself at odds with the Church, I understood on some level that Jesus was not responsible for what it had become, and it occurred to me he might ask some of the same questions I was asking about the hierarchy, intolerance, and fear of God that were promulgated in his name. Along with my questions about doctrine and dogma, I began to question what the dogma had to say about *him*. I decided I would try, for the first time, to get a perspective on Jesus that went beyond the Catholic view of him.

And setting out to learn more about Jesus brings up some pretty weighty questions.

Was Jesus a real historical figure?

Was he a Christian?

Did Jesus come to start a new religion?

Was he man or is he God?

Did he rise from the dead?

Was he born of a virgin?

What was Jesus' real name?

What did he teach?

Was he the only Son of God?

Even though it could be argued that more has been written about Jesus than any other individual in history, we actually know very little about most of Jesus' life. He was born in a humble setting, which has been depicted in the dramatic and widely familiar Nativity story, and he walked this earth for approximately 33 years. Jesus lived much of his life out of the public eye; we know of his birth, we learn of a small incident from around age 12, and then we hear nothing of his life until he began his ministry around the age of 30. We are told that he traveled the countryside of Judea healing, preaching, teaching, exorcising demons, and even demonstrating dominion over the elements. Then, several years into his controversial ministry, at the height of his popularity, he was sentenced to death and executed in a place called Calvary. It is reported that he rose bodily from the dead three days after his crucifixion and appeared to his followers. These are the basic points of Jesus' life and death, from which an organized theology has been formulated as the basis of the world's largest religion.

Most of what we know about Jesus comes from the Bible, but his historicity is corroborated by secular historians of that approximate time, most notably Cornelius Tacitus (57–117 CE), one of the great Roman historians, as well as the Jewish historian Flavius Josephus (37–101 CE), who would become a Roman citizen. There is little doubt or argument that a man from Nazareth named Yeshua, or Jesus, lived a controversial life and died a public death. Where the dispute heats up is over what he was and what he taught.

THE REFORMER AND THE RELIGION

The religion *about* Jesus is very different from the religion *of* Jesus. Jesus was a devout Jew who had a serious quarrel with what had become of the Jewish temple system; he believed that the high priests exploited the common people, and that Judaism had become mired in law and too insistent on conforming to it. Jesus was a reformer, perhaps even a revolutionary, who challenged the separation that the Hebrew hierarchy created between the faithful and God. He argued that the belief system had grown to emphasize observance over spirituality and no longer met the spiritual needs of the Jewish people. Jesus saw that the temple practices had ceased to be transformational and had become a transactional (almost commercial) enterprise. It is ironic that the Church created in his name has become even bigger and more hierarchical than the one he attempted to reform.

The religion formed in Jesus' name, Christianity, with its three major divisions, Roman Catholicism, Eastern Orthodoxy, and Protestantism, claims to possess the one and only Truth and asserts that any other ideas about deity and spirituality are false. Inflammatory labels in the Christian framework, like *blasphemy* and *heresy*, are attached to anything and anyone outside the approved Christian dogma about God and/or Jesus. Christianity teaches that without converting to its belief system a person is condemned, with no possibility of salvation. Catholicism goes further and teaches that even its Christian cousins (Protestants) possess only part of the Truth about the Divine and, by remaining outside the Church, are jeopardizing their salvation and full union with God.

This "Christian" belief system is the theology about Jesus, not necessarily the theology of Jesus. The religion based on the life and teaching of Jesus has been formulated, promulgated, enforced, and defended by perhaps the most powerful and wealthy private institution the world has ever known. To think that Jesus envisioned such a powerful, opulent, and, at times, ruthless institution seems an extreme distortion when we measure the religion it has become against the man himself. Jesus emphasized a simple and straightforward path to a relationship with God. The complexity of Christian doctrine seems altogether contrary to the simplicity of the historic Jesus. It is hard to envision the humility of Jesus within the opulence and pomp of Rome.

Jesus was not a Christian. In contrast to conventional Christian wisdom, it is doubtful Jesus came to start a new religion at all. But, if he had, the religion he started probably wouldn't have been as steeped in dogma and hierarchy as Christianity has become. Jesus complained bitterly about the rigid, hierarchical, dogmatic form that the religion of his ancestors had taken—yet after his death an even more complex and mysterious religion was formed in his name. The ensuing centuries saw splits and schisms that have multiplied to yield dozens of differing versions of Christianity, most claiming to possess the absolute truth of his teaching. The disagreements are mostly over institutional issues of doctrine and authority that have little, if anything, to do with the life and death of Jesus, the ostensible foundation of the faith.

Jesus was a teacher, a preacher, a healer, and a revolutionary who *challenged* rampant institutionalism. He was a reformist bent on agitating the external practices of Jewish theology and an enlightened mystic testifying to a "new" truth about man's nature. Jesus didn't come to make more laws; he came to strike a blow at those in place.

Jesus spoke in a language and style understandable to the relatively uneducated and unsophisticated people he preached to in his day. If a language of spiritual truth were available, Jesus would not have had to rely so heavily on metaphor and allegory, yet even today there are still no words in which Divine Truth can be wholly expressed. Human language simply can't articulate it, but Jesus expressed Truth by his actions and in parables that embodied rather than enunciated a profound understanding. The storytelling style

Jesus used left much of his teaching open for interpretation, and there were hundreds of disparate readings—until the Church claimed the sole authority of interpreting for itself.

After Jesus died, the Church set itself up as the sole arbiter of Jesus' meaning and codified his message into a fixed, immutable, and infallible Truth. This is not likely what Jesus had in mind. The interpretations that his followers made many centuries ago should continually evolve as new followers view his stories and actions with the ever-increasing capacity of the evolving human consciousness. Yet Christianity allows for little or no "evolution" in the understanding of Jesus' message.

Jesus pointed man in the direction of the Truth. Sadly, mankind has mistaken the pointer to the Truth for the Truth itself. By locking in on the nature of Jesus as the central tenet of its theology, the Church stymies the natural evolution of our ability to understand the Truth of his message. The Church has created mystery around the simplicity of Jesus' message and is reluctant now to advance human understanding of it. But the Church's conclusions about what Jesus was and what he taught were drawn at a time when mankind believed the world was flat, electricity would have been considered supernatural, and women were seen as defective males, to name just a few beliefs that our evolving consciousness has abolished. Like other religious belief systems of the world, the Church, by turning teaching into dogma, has stymied the spiritual growth of its adherents and locked the ever-evolving human consciousness into a mode of understanding two thousand years old.

THE CONSCIOUSNESS OF CHRIST

Jesus is called God, Servant, Lord, Savior, Christ, King, Shepherd, Teacher, Preacher, Rabbi, Immanuel, Son of God, Son of Man,

Lamb of God, and more. His name is commonly understood to be Jesus Christ, but his real name was simply Jesus of Nazareth. Actually, he would have responded to the name Yeshua, which is Aramaic, the language he and his disciples spoke; Jesus is a Latin translation. His name in Hebrew would be Joshua, and in Greek, the original language of the Bible, he would be called Ihsous. Christ is not his surname; it is a description meaning "Messiah" or "savior."

The Church's concept of Jesus *Christ* perpetuates the idea that God is "up there" and mankind is "down here," with a gap in between that Jesus *(the Christ)* alone bridges. But in fact, "Christ" is a description of a *state of consciousness* that Jesus believed was available to all men. It is an awareness of God's indwelling within man—every man, not just Jesus of Nazareth. Christ is a level of consciousness toward which Jesus encouraged us all to follow him. Jesus taught that we all have the potential to be Christ; that Christ is a state of being we can achieve through a connection to the mind of God using the individualized mind each of us possesses. Jesus was perhaps the most perfect example of the Christ potential in man; his fulfillment of this Christ consciousness is what gave him the powers he possessed. He discovered, more than any before him, and perhaps any after, that God lived inside him and was wholly available to him, even to the point of demonstrating "supernatural" power.

Jesus said of the miracles he was performing that he expected others to do even greater things after him. The idea that Infinite Intelligence (God) dwells within all men—the most basic and elemental Truth of the universe—that is the Truth that Jesus tried to exemplify and teach. All else takes shape under this Truth. But man formed a religion to worship Jesus instead, making him God rather than following his example to find God within us.

If a man or woman possessed or, more accurately, *achieved* the consciousness of Jesus, he or she might also heal the sick, raise the

dead, and have dominion over nature. Jesus was a man who found
the true and literal dwelling place of God; his mission was to lead
all men to the place where he knew God to reside. He called it the
Kingdom of Heaven, and he even told us where to find it: "The
kingdom of God does not admit of observation and there will be
no one to say, 'Look here! Look there!' For you must know the
kingdom of God is within you."[1]

We must keep in mind, as we consider the Christ consciousness, that while the *concept* of God is man-made, the *Truth* about
God is not. The Spirit of which Jesus spoke is not something that
can be expressed with human words or understood by the rational,
finite human mind. We can, however, *connect* to this Spirit through
the internal channels of our human mind, the only "place" we
can connect to the spiritual nature we all possess. We access God
through Christ because the Infinite God becomes individual in
each of us through the Christ potential we each possess.

THE ONE AND ONLY SON?

The primary tenet the Church teaches is that Jesus is the Son
of God. And not just that; he is the *only* Son of God. Church
doctrine says God sent his only son to earth for the benefit of
mankind, to bridge the gap between man and God created by
man's sinfulness. In the Nicene Creed, most Christians recite
that Jesus is "begotten, not made, one in being with the Father."
In theological terms, this way of coming into being is known as
the Incarnation. Jesus is not portrayed as an equal member of
the human race; he has a special and singular status, truly one
of a kind, completely human yet completely God. The Church
constantly reminds us that he is not actually one of us; he is
God, offered to mankind for worship and adoration; he is above

man in the divine hierarchy; his connection to God is a singular event. Jesus is theologically situated between man and God (actually, *seated* at the right hand of the Father) to advocate for us with Him.

Prayers, hymns, and Catechism state redundantly that Jesus is the "only Son of God," and adjacent to this idea is the reminder that we are not. We are somehow different from Jesus, we are separated from God, and Jesus' mission is to bridge the gap. Christians learn that mankind is not able, actually not *worthy*, to reach God without the intercession of Jesus. And the Church claims that it is acting on behalf of and with the authority of Jesus, so mankind cannot reach God except through the intercession of the Church. Does this sound right to you? Did Jesus come to place a new institution between mankind and God, or did he come to show mankind the way to "the Kingdom of Heaven"?

On several occasions Jesus does in fact say that he is the Son of God. The question is whether he claims this status exclusively, saying that he *alone* is the Son of God, the singular, the one and only. Does Jesus' claim to be the Son of God match the claim the Church makes for him? (Not according to the Gnostics.)

Let's look at how the Catechism describes Jesus: "The unique and altogether singular event of the Incarnation of the Son of God does not mean that Jesus Christ is part God and part man, nor does it imply that he is the result of a confused mixture of the Divine and the human. He became truly man while remaining truly God. Jesus Christ is true God and true man."[2]

The phrase to take special note of here is "the unique and altogether singular event." Here the Church is stating clearly that Jesus is the only man ever born with true divinity in his nature. It states with certitude that Jesus' nature is very different from ours. His "Incarnation" is a "singular event."

The Church teaches five distinct points about Jesus as the Son of God: 1. That at the time in history appointed by God, His only son was incarnated as an individual man, and that without losing his divine nature (and stature) he assumed a human nature. 2. That Jesus was true God and true man in the unified nature of his divine person, and for this reason Jesus is the singular (one and only) mediator between God and mankind. 3. That Jesus possesses two natures, one divine and the other human. These two natures are not in conflict, nor are they "confused," but united in one person. 4. That Jesus, being God and man, has human intelligence and will, in perfect harmony with and influenced by the divine intelligence and will he has in common with God. 5. That, finally, "the Incarnation is therefore the mystery of the wonderful union of the divine and human natures in the one person."

Where does this doctrine come from? The Bible does not delve into such complex explanations of Jesus' nature, and Jesus himself keeps it notably simpler. These teachings are conclusions arrived at through much theological debate over several centuries, yet the Church claims to find them right in the teaching of Jesus.

One rationale often given to "prove" that Jesus claims singular sonship looks to the Gospel scene when he stands trial. He is being peppered with questions intended to "catch" him in blasphemy. When Pilate asks him directly if he is the "Son of God," Jesus answers similarly in three of the four Gospels: "The words are your own"[3]; "I am"[4]; or "It is you who say that I am."[5] Only one of these statements makes an explicit claim to be the Son of God; the other two don't deny it. But do any of them convey exclusivity? Do they state unequivocally that Jesus is God? Do these statements create a distance between him and us?

If Jesus had a strong claim to make, wouldn't he have done so now? Why would he be taciturn at such an important moment?

He knew his time was at hand; if his most important theological message was about his nature, that he was God, he could have driven it home here. He was claiming to be the Son of God, but was he claiming it for himself alone? He was affirming his own divinity, but was he denying mine, or yours? Perhaps, in keeping with most of the other things he taught, he was not pointing us away from God, nor was he inserting himself between man and God. Jesus never denies the divine aspect of our human nature by demonstrating his own divinity.

Elsewhere in the Bible we find Jesus making references to sonship earlier in his life. "Everything has been entrusted to me by my father,"[6] he says, and at another point, "No one knows the Son except the Father, just as no one knows the Father except the Son and those to whom the Son chooses to reveal him."[7] This may be the closest Jesus comes to stating that he is in fact God. But even here he does not claim sonship exclusively. Jesus speaks a distinct language of unity—unity that describes his relationship to *his* Father and our own relationship with *our* Father as well.

The sense of duality, or separation from God, comes through in the language of the Church, supported by the dense verbiage of dogma, but *not* in the words of Jesus. On the contrary, he claims we are all sons and daughters of God. A prevalent motif in Church teaching is humanity's unworthiness to commune directly with God. Did Jesus come to show us how to heal, or did he come to install an institution on earth as the only way for us to heal?

A WINDOW IN THE WALL

The difficulty with Church teaching on the exclusive sonship of Jesus is that it creates duality that it seems clear Jesus didn't intend. Of course Jesus is the Son of God, but if Jesus is the *only* Son of

God, what am I? What are *you*? Aren't we all sons and daughters of the Creator we call God? Doesn't Jesus emphasize the commonality between himself and us? To claim that Jesus is both true man and God makes him into something unique, separate from the rest of us. It creates an unreasonable expectation of us to attain what he discovered for us: do you have to be true God and true man in order to find the Kingdom? Wasn't he saying the Kingdom is available to us all?

At Santa Maria we were taught that mankind had become separated from God by the action of Adam and Eve in the Garden of Eden. Man, exercising his free will, lost the union he enjoyed with God. Jesus came to restore that union, but he was not the bridge over the gap; he was showing us how to close the gap. Jesus made a discovery: he found where God dwelt and he was passionate and fearless about sharing his discovery with us, attempting to point us in the direction of God. Jesus discovered a new and unique relationship to the Infinite Mind we call God, and he began to access this Infinite Intelligence to exist in a metaphysical plane that few, if any, besides him have been able to do. *Jesus achieved Christ consciousness.*

Just because the rest of humanity does not easily attain this metaphysical awareness does not negate his teaching that we are all capable of feats equal to and even greater than his own. Why would Jesus say this if he weren't expressing in no uncertain terms that what he has achieved, all of us can attain? That he is just opening the gate, and he expects even stronger expressions of divinity from us?

To say that we are men in the same class as Jesus is not exactly true; Jesus overcame the human part of himself that keeps mankind separated from God. But Jesus was opening a door for us to discover our own individualized expressions of God as well. When he talked about the Kingdom of Heaven, this is what he meant. The

Kingdom of Heaven is not a place where we go. When Jesus commands us to follow him, it is to a place of higher consciousness, not to some esoteric place above the clouds. *The Kingdom is not a place of being, it is a state of being.* It is the consciousness of God that we access through the portal of our own individual human consciousness.

Author Eric Butterworth speaks of man's separation from God as a "middle wall of partition" in which Jesus created a breach: "He created a window in the wall, a great picture window through which man can view the vast and beautiful panorama of the spiritual dimension of life."[8] Jesus pointed *through* the window; he didn't point to himself. The Church has assumed the position of the window and blocked our view. More and more we have been directed to look *at* the window instead of *through* it.

Thanks to the Church, Jesus became the object of man's focus instead of the lens for focus he intended to become. But the window Butterworth refers to is intended to be seen through, not looked at: "Millions upon millions of devotees through the ages have come and knelt before this window, but occasionally does a clear-minded thinker clean the darkened glass and see through the window.... Anyone may wipe away the dusty concepts and have a firsthand and immediate experience of unity with God. You may know the Truth and find your freedom to become what God has created you to be."[9] Butterworth goes further and claims that we should resist the historical tendency to worship Jesus; when he becomes an object of our worship, he ceases to be our leader, the pointer he believed himself to be.

We don't know if Jesus' discovery of nonduality was gradual or instantaneous. We only know that when his time came to begin teaching he was more than ready to discuss it. He had already made the discovery of his nature and was ready to point us all in the direction he knew as Truth.

BORN OF A VIRGIN

In Christian doctrine, the very birth of Jesus sets him apart from us. Much is made of the circumstances: the Bible tells us that Mary became pregnant with Jesus either by the Holy Spirit (Matthew) or by the shadow of God (Luke). Two direct references in the New Testament state that he was born of a virgin (Matthew 1:18 and Luke 1:26).

The idea of a superior being, part man and part god, was nothing new in theology. There is considerable precedent in other religious belief systems for such a being and for the Virgin Birth as well. Buddha, Krishna, the Pharaohs, and many figures from Greek mythology were reportedly born of collaboration between the human and the Divine. One difference between Jesus' birth and the virgin births in pagan religions before him, though, is that many other mythologies have a male deity involved in the physical act of conception, while Jesus' conception is reported to be enacted by the Holy Spirit or a shadow of God, not the physical presence of God.

Why insist on these special circumstances for Jesus' conception and birth? The Church likely had its own reasons, theological and doctrinal, for the virgin-birth scenario. A natural birth, the common birth that all humans experience, was not enough for Jesus if the theology about Jesus was going to make him God.

The Virgin Birth creates a separation between Jesus and the rest of mankind that perpetuates the duality of the belief system. It also implies a message about the human act of procreation: that process is not pure enough to give rise to the Son of God, even though the son is to be considered fully human. Mary must remain "pure" in order to give birth to this unique child. The obvious implication is that all other humans brought into this world are in the most basic way impure.

If God decided to impregnate a virgin, being omnipotent, He certainly could if He wanted to. The question is not whether God could impregnate a virgin; the question is *why would He?* God likely plays a role in some way in everyone's conception; God is the Source of life for all that is created, so why would He need to take over the process altogether in the case of Jesus? Why would he contribute to the duality, the separation between man and God, if He intended Jesus to eliminate it?

We cannot presume to know the mind of God, but even from a purely strategic point of view, if the salvation of mankind is the primary motive to "send" Jesus into the world, doesn't sending a *human* make more sense than sending a *god?* "God as man" buttresses the wall of partition, whereas "man as God" creates an opening to a new way of thinking—a new consciousness and a new covenant between God and His creation. If Jesus came to save man, he would do a better job *as* a man. If he really came to lead us to salvation and not to *be our salvation,* he would best lead from the front of the pack, not from above.

There are a few other biblical and doctrinal anomalies that we should consider as we probe this particular mystery of faith— the one that really got my attention back in grade school, much to the dismay of the nuns. The Catholic Church claims that Mary remained a virgin *post partum,* that is, after Jesus was born and throughout the rest of her life. Interestingly, the Bible never claims this; instead, it clearly refers to Jesus' brothers and sisters, particularly James, who became the first bishop of Jerusalem. Protestants believe Mary was a virgin until after Jesus' birth and then lived a quite normal Jewish life of procreation, which was an important duty to all Jews of that time. The Catholic version of events holds that Mary was a virgin throughout her life and that the reference to Jesus' siblings means sons of another Mary, a disciple of Christ, or other children Joseph had before he married Mary. This is a liberty of explanation taken by Church leaders, not the Gospel writers.

Another notable conundrum arises in both Matthew and Luke, the only two Gospel authors who speak of the Virgin Birth, when they offer accounts of Jesus' ancestry. According to both, Jesus was born in the bloodline of King David as prophesied in the Old Testament. Jesus is quoted as saying the same himself in the Book of Revelation: "I am of David's line, the root of David and the bright star of the morning."[10] Both Matthew and Luke trace the bloodline from Jewish antiquity directly through Joseph, not Mary. This evidence is circumstantial, perhaps, but why is it presented at all? Does it contradict the doctrine that Joseph was not party to Jesus' conception? Is it a hint that the genealogy of Jesus may be more important to the prophecy than the details of the conception are? Why did the same writers who wrote about a Virgin Birth also give us the genealogy that creates such a discrepancy? If Mary is a virgin, Jesus is not in the bloodline of David; if Jesus is in the bloodline of David, Mary is not a virgin.

Finally, there's another, more pragmatic issue that may be a factor in the Virgin Birth mythology—a bit of ancient gossip, if you will. It had been rumored, starting in Jesus' hometown of Nazareth, that Jesus was illegitimate, that he was conceived out of wedlock. To the early Church leaders it would have been unacceptable to have the figurehead of the new movement be conceived out of wedlock—it would be too cumbersome an issue to explain away—so the concept of divine intervention, quite possibly borrowed from other theological movements, was brought in to explain the birth of Jesus and at the same to bolster the theology of God Incarnate.

HIS LIFE IN THE WORLD

For us kids at Santa Maria, as for most Catholic students, teaching about the central figure of our religion focused mostly on the Baby Jesus, who came into the world in such a picturesque and humble way, and the Resurrected Christ Jesus, who died for our sins in such an ignominious and ghastly way. What can we learn about his purpose and his message from the things that happened in between? Two of the four Gospel writers, Matthew and Luke, tell slightly differing stories about the birth of Jesus; the other two, Mark and John, don't mention his birth at all. One of the Gospels (Luke) tells a story in which 12-year-old Jesus lingers behind after a family visit to Jerusalem. For three days, Jesus converses with scholars and teachers in the temple, where he impresses them with his wisdom. When his parents find him, Jesus mildly rebuffs their scolding as he makes his first reference to his "Father" and his mission. "'My child, why have you done this to us? See how worried your father and I have been, looking for you.' 'Why were you looking for me?' he replied. 'Did you not know that I must be busy with my Father's affairs?' But they did not understand what he meant." Luke is indicating that Jesus knew of his stature and of his calling by age 12, if not sooner. But Jesus then returns to Nazareth, not to be heard from again until his cousin John baptizes him when he is around 30 years old. This is where Mark and John pick up the story.

Where did Jesus spend the 18 years between this incident and "going public" after his baptism? One intriguing speculation is that Jesus spent those years studying and teaching in India. There is obviously no proof of this account beyond some titillating coincidences reportedly found in ancient journals discovered in Tibet about a saint called Issa. Another popular myth is that he went to England, and some stories speculate that he even traveled to America. Most scholars, however, believe that Jesus stayed at home with his parents and probably worked with Joseph as a carpenter.

One thing seems certain about Jesus, though: when he finally became a public figure, he was well prepared for the work that he would do for the rest of his short life. He was a gifted speaker and a wise teacher who attracted a growing following as he traveled Judea. Somehow, Jesus became abundantly equipped to excel at his work. He was a dynamic leader, a knowledgeable biblical scholar, and a charismatic orator.

After he was baptized, Jesus is reported to have performed many miracles, his first at a wedding at Cana where he changed water into wine when the host's supply ran out. Over the next three years, he healed various illnesses, raised people from the dead, calmed stormy seas, fed large crowds with scanty provisions, and walked on water, among other supernatural feats. The Gospels recount more than 30 miracles of Jesus and there were probably many more not recorded. (Interestingly, the account in Tibet reports Issa performing healing miracles there as well.)

In the political sphere, Jesus would have been controversial, to say the least. He spoke out against the Jewish temple system and the commercial enterprise it had become. He was an anti-establishment figure—we'd call him a populist today—who challenged the status quo and ruffled many feathers in the process. He was a champion of the downtrodden and defender of the lowly. He didn't betray his "blue-collar" background, and this is one of the reasons why he is thought to have stayed in his home region during the so-called missing years: he showed no sign of being an elite or educated aristocrat, such as a world traveler might have exhibited. Jesus was a provincial figure with a human view of the spiritual world, not a refined elitist with a worldly view of human spirituality.

In the end, he was arrested and tried by his own people and nailed to a wooden cross under the authority of Pilate, the Roman governor. Then, after three days, he rose from the dead and appeared to his disciples. He reportedly remained on earth for 40 days and then bodily ascended into Heaven.

Jesus' life was foretold in Scripture in passages that promised the coming of a savior, a Messiah, but there was some confusion as to the form in which this Messiah would come. The Jews had been awaiting his arrival for centuries; they believed the Messiah would come as a conquering hero. Jesus made his appearance as a humble servant. Naturally enough, many people concluded from this that he was not the Messiah at all.

What did Jesus himself conclude? The nuns at Santa Maria taught us that he knew from birth that he was God. Is it more likely that he discovered his divinity during his lifetime? Let's look more closely at his awareness in hopes of expanding our own.

THE DISCOVERY

It is entirely plausible, even probable, that Jesus, at some point during his life as an adolescent or young adult, made The Discovery. Perhaps this is the meaning of the story told by Luke about Jesus at the age of 12 at the temple in Jerusalem. Whether or not he is the "only Son of God, sent down from Heaven," he certainly possessed a greater awareness of his innate divinity than any other human before or (probably) since. He discovered the Divine within himself and he called it the Kingdom of Heaven. He found his God nature and invited all of mankind to "follow" him in this discovery. Nobody knows if the discovery was gradual or instantaneous, but we do know that when he began his ministry, he was fully aware of his divinity. He knew he was an individual expression of the Infinite One, which he called "Father."

Jesus never claimed sole possession of the discovery or the powers he demonstrated through his use of it. In fact, he predicted that his followers would do feats greater than his own. He expected an evolution of spirituality that unfortunately has not yet come, at least not to any great degree. Why hasn't it happened the way Jesus anticipated? Because he was made into an object of worship before his real message could take root. Mankind, directed by the Church, ignored Jesus' message to look within for spiritual truth and passed along a tradition of looking to Jesus as Truth instead. Rather than following his example to make our own discoveries, we have enshrined *his* personal discovery as the basis of our belief and the endpoint of our search. We miss his most important lesson.

Jesus' objective was to show the *natural man* that the source of the *spiritual man* he had been searching for was within reach. In fact, it was so close that all it took was an enlightened man such as him to point us in the right direction. If we strip away all the layers of theological "enrichment" from the words of Jesus, we see that salvation is a practice, not a belief; it is an experience, not a ritualized formula of complex dogma. *Jesus taught a "religion" of transformation, not one of transaction.*

Unless and until we grasp this primary point of Jesus' discovery, we as individuals, like the Church as a whole, stay mired in a system based on belief in doctrine and never truly experience the reality of divinity Jesus pointed us toward. In Eric Butterworth's words, "We must see Jesus as the great discoverer of the Divinity of Man, the pioneer and way-shower in the great world of the within. . . . When He becomes the object of our worship, He ceases to be the way-shower for our own self-realization and self-unfoldment."[11]

A KINGDOM IN THE CLOUDS?

Until Jesus, man lived distinctly separate from God. There was man on one side of the "veil" and God on the other. Jesus pierced the veil, eliminated the partition between man and his Creator. Jesus, through his enlightenment, eliminated duality.

When he worked miracles, he wasn't just parading his special skills. Jesus was a teacher, not a performer. He may have had outstanding performance skills that he used to teach, but he certainly didn't just perform for the sake of impressing his followers. When he demonstrated his dominion over nature and his ability to heal, he did so to set an example for his followers. To believe otherwise would be to place Jesus in the grotesque role of a wizard or magician. Why would Jesus just *perform* miracles? To prove he was God? To keep mankind in its lowly place? To show off? No, Jesus was *demonstrating* the power he accessed through his own individual discovery of his divinity. Teaching by example is what the very best teachers do.

Jesus was showing us the path to our own salvation, our own individual expression of divinity. Jesus came to share his exaltation with us, to demonstrate how to live through this divine nature he had discovered. In the passage we mentioned earlier, he says: "It is the Father, living in me, who is doing this work. You must believe me when I say that I am in the Father and the Father is in me; believe it on the evidence of this work if for no other reason. I tell you most solemnly, whoever believes in me will perform the same works as I do myself, he will perform even greater works."[12] This is a powerful statement of the purpose of Jesus' ministry—to teach us to have *faith* in our divinity. He is explaining that his works are for the sole purpose of demonstrating his divinity ("the Father is in me"), and he clearly invites his followers to perform even greater feats. Jesus is telling mankind that he is just the beginning, that in his wake he wishes for others to "perform" miracles beyond the ones he has done. He is imploring man to simply "believe" in his own divinity as well.

Jesus intended to teach that all of mankind had, within each individual, the divine spark of God. He wanted us to realize that not only was *he* God individualized, *each of us is God individualized too!* The omnipotent nature of God is in all men and all men are within Him. Jesus wasn't trying to show how different he was from us; he was trying to get us to have faith that we were just like him.

Jesus invited us to the Kingdom of Heaven. Exactly where is this Kingdom? Is it "up there" above the clouds, as Christian theology would have us imagine? Clearly, Jesus was inviting us to follow him on a journey of personal discovery, not a journey into the upper atmosphere. The journey Jesus takes us on leads us *inside,* to the place where he found his power to conquer nature and to heal the sick. It's important to note that Jesus didn't simply touch those he healed; he spoke in an affirmative way and commanded healing *through the faith of the one being healed.* Jesus understood that God was able to incarnate Himself millions of times over, infinitely and simultaneously, through His creation. Jesus called on God, actually *commanded* God, to heal the person he was speaking to. He used the power that already existed within that person to perform the healing. He called on God to perform the healing from the "Kingdom" *within* the person. He showed us the power to heal ourselves.

Mankind is a personification of God, individualized in every person born into this world. Each individual is an outlet for the Divine. It is this potential in man that Jesus realized and, like the shepherd he so often referred to in his stories, was trying to lead us to.

He brought a simple message that the Church then intellectualized, formalized, and institutionalized into a theology only the learned were able to grasp. His message, dogmatized and doctrinized, is frozen in antiquity. The deposit of faith Jesus made into human consciousness was converted into doctrine two millennia ago in accord with the capacity of human understanding at that time, and that understanding remains largely intact today, with no way to expand or evolve.

THE EMPTY TOMB

The doctrine of the Church places its greatest emphasis of all on Jesus' resurrection from the dead. In dying and rising, we are told, Jesus opens the gates of Heaven for us all.

There it is again—the duality of the teaching. The idea that we are here and that we are trying to get somewhere else and that we need help from some other party to gain access. Jesus gives us access to Heaven and the Church gives us access to Jesus.

In fact, Jesus rising from the dead demonstrates what he really preached: that mankind has a divine and spiritual nature. The power of his faith in this truth allowed him to demonstrate the spiritual essence that exists within the physical body. There must have been a point in the process of his crucifixion where he completely overcame the physical death his body was enduring. If it is true that we are spiritual beings, that we embody some of the spirit of God, and that this spirit is some form of energy, then the energy that fuels our physical existence, our life force, must be transmuted into something else when our physical body expires. With the extremely high awareness of his God nature that he had achieved, Jesus (we may speculate) was able to either reenter the corpse or, more likely, to appear in an ethereal state in which his spirit was strong enough to be visible to others still in the physical plane.

What happened to Jesus' body? The Church teaches that he rose from the tomb and then he ascended bodily "up" to Heaven. The idea of Jesus raising his body doesn't pose problems for me, but the idea that he ascended into the sky, to Heaven, perpetuates the myth of duality. I think it makes more sense that Jesus did indeed ascend to another plane of existence, and that from this "resurrected" state he sent out a very strong stream of consciousness—the Christ consciousness—for his "followers" to tap into. This is why Jesus is still alive for those who follow him. That we can tap into the stream of consciousness of Jesus is a powerful reality for us to discover and experience.

Jesus, being more God-like than the rest, realized that his confinement to a physical body was temporary. This awareness allowed him to remain composed and faithful throughout the physical ordeal he endured. And this is what his example means for us. *He wasn't teaching us to suffer;* he was teaching that with God dwelling within, *we could overcome suffering*—even the grotesque suffering he endured on the physical plane.

The empty tomb in and of itself doesn't prove that Jesus rose from the dead as historical fact. It is a necessary sign, however. If his body had remained in the tomb, would his resurrection be impossible? Not really—only in the way the Church teaches it, because the doctrine holds that the physical body is resurrected. Jesus needs to rise from the tomb to make a different point.

Jesus raised others from the dead during his own lifetime, and these actions were considered miracles. The subjects Jesus raised resumed life as they knew it before. *Jesus does not.* When Jesus rises, it is a different "resurrection" than, for example, that of Lazarus. Lazarus shrugged off his shroud and went about his business, presumably none the worse for his four days entombed. After Jesus rises, He displays to his disciples the wounds of his torture and death, showing that he has the same body he had in life. But, at the same time, he distinctly shows "new properties of a glorious body."[13] He walks through doors, appears, and disappears; he is no longer bound by space or time: "The doors were closed, but Jesus came in and stood among them."[14] There is something different about his presence, too; several times his disciples fail to recognize him. His body is glorified, as one would expect a body to be after coming into direct contact with the Divine. Jesus' awareness of his divinity is being rewarded and displayed for all to see. *This* is the example Jesus is setting for us: that the spirit of God within a human being, once reunited with God, becomes complete and whole and overcomes all physical limitations, even death itself.

The death at Calvary is necessary because it is so obvious. It challenges his followers' faith and discourages them deeply. Right up to the end, they expect Jesus to overcome the men who are killing him by coming down from the Cross before he dies. He *does* overcome those who killed him—and the result of their actions as well—not by making a dramatic escape, but by overcoming death itself. If he had simply prevented his death from occurring, it would have been another "miracle" performed by a superhuman being. But by undergoing death, a very public and obvious death, and then overcoming it, he was demonstrating his real divinity. He wasn't just acting as a healer by channeling God, he was showing he was divine, and by use of the metaphor of opening the gates, he was telling us that we were too. He didn't "open the gates" to any place outside us; he opened a way within. He was showing by example that our destiny, too, is to overcome death. When we die, if we have just a measure of the faith in our own divinity that Jesus had, we too will exist on a plane where we can transcend time and space. This is eternity: a place where time and space do not exist.

This is where we are to follow Jesus. We are not going to a place, but to a state, just like him.

Jesus didn't start another belief system; he challenged the one he was born into. He believed that the Jewish hierarchy had created a belief system that was too laden with laws and had strayed too far, too long, from the spiritual experience of Moses, Abraham, and the prophets. Jesus made a discovery of divinity within himself, a discovery he invited us all to follow him toward. He taught about the kingdom of Heaven, but it is clear he was not speaking of a place apart from where we are now, a place where God dwells apart from us. He was pointing to the Kingdom within each of us where God resides.

Jesus was so evolved, it's really no wonder that his followers worshipped him as God. It's easy to see why they built a religion in his honor and became so very dependent upon him for their own salvation. But it seems likely that Jesus would repudiate the complex doctrinal system set up in his honor every bit as firmly as he did the institutionalization of his beloved, native Judaism.

If Jesus came today, what would he think of the doctrine of infallibility, the rigid hierarchy, Saint Peter's Basilica in Rome, the opulent wealth of the Church? What would he make of the grandiose titles its leaders have bestowed upon themselves, the custom and costume of the Church? What would he think about things the Church has done in his name—the Crusades, the Inquisition, the tacit condoning of the Holocaust? What would he say about the texts that were chosen to make up the Bible—would he think they told his story truly? Would he approve of the complicated form in which doctrine was laid down several hundred years after he left us and then preserved, untouched, for centuries more?

Would Jesus feel at home in the Vatican?

THIRTEEN

DISCERNING
THE DIVINE

OUT OF THE WORLD
AND INTO THE WOODS

I closed on the sale of the *Daily News* in April 2000. I could now
live up to my end of The Deal, made a little more than 20 years
earlier in late 1979. Everything I had succeeded or failed at, every
person I had come in contact with, every bit of synchronicity, luck,
and serendipity, all of the courage and all of the fear, all the guidance, help, and inspiration I received along the way had conspired
to bring me to this point. I didn't have an inkling of doubt that
my situation now was the work of the other party in The Deal. The
ball was now in my court. Would I live up to my end of The Deal?

Yes, as daunting as it seemed at the time, I would try with everything I had. But how did one keep this kind of bargain? Where
would I begin? My end of it was vague from the start. I felt responsible for sharing some insight I still wasn't even sure I had.

But the change in my life was a shock to my system. I was accustomed to facing down daily deadlines, conducting strategic meetings, and rendering my opinion on the affairs of the world. I had
over a hundred employees, more than ten thousand loyal readers,
two thousand advertisers, and a handful of politicians on speed

dial. One moment I was thriving in an exciting and successful publishing career, and the next moment—well, I wasn't.

IDENTITY CRISIS

On Thursday I'm the publisher and owner of a growing suburban newspaper group, by Monday I'm nothing. I have no role, no title, no responsibilities, no deadlines, and, really, no position in society. Wait! No title? No role? No deadlines? No job?! *Hey, hold on a minute! I love my job!* Being the publisher of a daily newspaper is one of the coolest jobs in this country. I was proud and gratified to be one of only about a thousand fortunate people in the United States who could call themselves daily newspaper publishers. That romance I'd felt all those years ago about selling ad space in support of the Fourth Estate just multiplied as I climbed. I believed then, and still do today, that I was the CEO of the finest, most talented, best-trained, and most courageous daily newspaper staff in the country and that being their torchbearer was a privilege.

With 13 years in newspapering under my belt, I was growing into my role as leader of this group and a community leader as well. I was maturing, finally able to relax and truly relish my work, maybe for the first time ever. I was involved in everything happening in town, I got to opine every day about whatever I wanted—local issues, national events, international crisis—no topic in the *world* was off limits. I was one of the lucky ones who woke up early and charged to the office, not because of anxiety or fear of losing my job, but because I *loved* my job. I was addicted to the action: deadlines, editorial meetings, lunches with movers and shakers, chairman of this, trustee of that. I had input, prestige, vital work, and a very comfortable income. My life was full and exciting on almost every level.

I turned over a lot more than the keys to the office when I signed the contract. When I turned over those keys, how was I to know I was giving up all of the roles that made up my self-image? Nothing had prepared me for this type of loss. Mostly because I'd had solid and specific goals, I always thought I knew who I was and where I was headed, but without a distinct role, I was headed for an unexpected crisis of identity.

I thought I was selling a physical asset at a great monetary profit, but I never considered I'd bartered some part of me in the deal as well. How was I to know my self-image was somewhere in that little daily newspaper? I loved my work and the *Daily News,* to be sure, but I never felt all that attached to it when I did own it; I was merely caught up in the work, or so I thought. I simply seized a business opportunity on the front end (bought it cheap) and capitalized on it on the back end (sold it at a premium). I loved every second of that exciting and rewarding life, but it was just a means to an end, right? It was a vehicle to get me to one more goal.

I had the chance I'd been dreaming of, the chance I knew was coming all along, the chance to cash in and walk away. Could I turn my back on the business deal and ignore The Deal? Dare I even think about it? In fact, I was briefly tempted to walk away from the sale and hang on to the wonderful life I had built as The Publisher. But I knew what I had to do. I went through the motions of weighing this decision, but I wasn't fooling anybody; I was not going to ignore this very real opportunity to change the direction of my life. There were plenty of reasons to sell, but the biggest was this: I couldn't—wouldn't—turn away from The Deal. All those years, knowing somehow I'd find myself in this position when I turned 40, I believed I'd be risking the wrath of the other party to The Deal—whoever or whatever that was.

Not knowing any other young people who had cashed out, I had no role model for the new role life had just "rewarded" me with. I had no role, no identity, and no peers to commiserate and play with, either. I had no preparation for this kind of a life, so I began to drift—at first, just a little. The first decision I made was not to go back to work too quickly. (That was easy—though maybe not too smart.) I would keep my hands busy but leave lots of time for decompressing as I planned the next era of my life. I was going to shift from "success to significance," as Bob Buford touts in his book *Halftime*. I was going to do something bigger, something more important than merely making money. I just wasn't sure what.

SQUARING THE DEAL

I was still operating on the assumption that I had made The Deal with the Church, so that's where I turned first. I thought I would reciprocate by offering myself to the Church in a very literal way.

We closed the newspaper deal on a Thursday, and on Monday morning I was sitting in one of the offices of the Archdiocese of Kansas City, ready to render services of their choosing. I had made an 8:30 appointment with the director of Catholic Charities and I was excited to begin living up to my end of The Deal. All of my training told me that the only connection I could make with God was through the Church, despite the doubts about its dogma that had nagged at me over the years and the glimpses I'd had of a more personal and transformative spirituality. So here I was, knocking on the door of the Church with freshly deposited millions and a real sense of indebtedness. The very best kind of Catholic, right? I wasn't factoring in the real and tangible evidence my life had shown me to the contrary; I was convinced that the Church was the place for me to be at that moment in my life. To me, the Catholic Church was God's only legitimate worldly representative.

I had encountered a spiritual presence at the tender age of 20 that led me to live my life in the expectation of worldly success that would, in turn, afford me the opportunity—as well as the responsibility—to communicate an as yet undetermined message of spiritual connection. The expectations had come to fruition and now I wanted to dispense with the responsibility part—my part. So here I was, sitting in a conference room, filling out a questionnaire and being grilled by the director's assistant. I explained that I had a lot of organizational experience but I was willing to get on a truck and deliver refrigerators to the poor if that was what they needed me to do. I wanted to be a humble servant, and I would fill any void they might have had at the time. The assistant to the director explained that the director was busy but asked me to wait.

So I waited. And waited some more. I waited for nearly three and a half hours. At 11:45, I left without seeing either the director or his assistant again. My ego had begun screaming at me to leave after waiting about 15 minutes; after all, I was not only the publisher, I was now the rich former publisher, and part of me craved this acknowledgement. But I quieted down my ego's voice. Hours later, when the calm voice that I'd met years before on my trek to Texas also told me to leave, I did. By this time, I trusted this "sixth sense" in an instinctual, automatic way.

I left and never looked back. I never went back or even called back, and I thought it was their loss. I didn't make a scene, which was a little unlike me at the time; I didn't tell anyone off or demand that someone pay attention to me, I just slipped out the door, hopped in my car, and headed for the golf course. By 1:00 that afternoon, I was the newest member at an out-of-the-way little golf club about 20 minutes out my front door.

I was offended and a little confused by my visit to the Archdiocese, but I got over it pretty quickly. I chalked it up to typical Catholic institutional ineptness and forgot about the incident for a while. No big deal. Eventually, though, I'd start to wonder what would have happened had I met with the director that day. Would I have been on a truck by that afternoon? Would I have made a million-dollar donation and considered The Deal squared?

DYING TO BE A CATHOLIC

Less than two months later, I was standing in an intensive care unit in a hospital in San Diego, watching my father fight for life. He had been in Chicago, struggling to recover from a hip replacement, and by the time the doctors discovered he had been stricken with a life-threatening infection during the surgery, it was probably too late. Nevertheless, they reopened the hip to clean the infection out of him, and it seemed for a while he was going to recover. He left for his second home in San Diego to convalesce in those warm, soothing climes. He hadn't been there more than a few days when we got the call that he was in the hospital, gravely ill from the sepsis that was invading his organs through his infected blood. My three brothers and I were soon gathered around his bed as he faded in and out of consciousness. With our various asinine sibling animosities, some we'd held on to since boyhood, it had been years since we were all together.

At first we hoped he might survive this catastrophic attack on his system, but soon it became obvious that it was unlikely he would recover to any type of life he would be interested in living. It was a heartbreaking moment when he opened his eyes at one point, surveyed the room, and smiled the familiar smile only he possessed. My dad was still the most handsome of the five of us and his boyish, mischievous smile could melt a glacier. He looked at us and quipped, "So, this is what it takes to get the four of you in the same room?" We all chuckled, but I sensed we all felt a little guilty about the childish estrangements we'd carried for so long. I think we four brothers knew at this moment that we had disappointed our dying father in a way we could only understand now that we were parents ourselves. For many years he'd been dying to get his sons to reconcile; now his dying was the first step.

After a few days, with the outcome becoming clear, my three brothers all had to return to Chicago to tend to work and family. Since I had fewer demands (remember, no job?), I was the one who remained in San Diego to keep vigil and to help my dad's wife, Marge, who was aging and ailing too, set up home care for herself and get to and from the hospital. I was to meet with the doctors each day and report any news to my brothers back in Chicago.

One morning I came back from visiting a home-care provider and found Marge in my dad's ICU room with a young Catholic priest. "Oh, no, Father," I heard her say. "He can't receive Last Rites—he's been excommunicated from the Catholic Church." The young priest looked dumbfounded but seemed reluctant to press the issue. He was probably scared to inquire what heinous act my dad could possibly have committed to require such radical action on the part of the Church.

"What's going on?" I asked.

Marge turned to me. "I was just explaining to Father that your dad was kicked out of the Church because we got married."

I didn't want to upset my unconscious father or his feeble and bewildered wife, so I invited the priest outside. I actually held him firmly by the arm, just above the elbow, the way Sister Mary Alice had held mine so many times so many years before.

I was still gripping his arm when I snarled at him, mere inches from his face, "You *know* better than this, Father. You go back into that room, you explain to that poor woman the truth about this excommunication bullshit, and you give my father his last rites! And do it *now!* And one more thing—if he's still alive tomorrow, do it again!"

"Of course, Mr. O'Donnell, of course," he stammered. "And I, I am so very sorry."

I stood trembling with anger and sorrow at the door while the young priest tenderly explained to my dad's wife that her husband was indeed a Catholic, that "once a Catholic, always a Catholic," and that whoever had told him otherwise was wrong. She kept asking, "Are you sure, Father? Are you sure?" I'm not sure if he convinced her, but she was relieved that her husband received his last rites and was indeed going to die a Catholic.

But my dad never regained consciousness, so he never knew it. His body was flown back to Chicago, where he had a proper funeral Mass in the Little Chapel across the street from the main church at Santa Maria in Mundelein. He now rests in a Catholic Cemetery in suburban Chicago near his brothers and his mom.

Now my problem with dogma was personal. I was pissed. What kind of a religion closes its doors against a man in the last hours of his life, letting him think that his God has rejected him because of a rule he broke? It still hurts to realize that my dad lived out the last 20-plus years of his life afraid to set foot into a Catholic church, where he had found so much solace during some rough patches in his life. How must this gregarious Irish Catholic have felt about being shut out that way? How much guilt must he have been harboring just for finding happiness in marriage? I really don't know; we never discussed it. I didn't know of his belief until that day in the ICU. If I had known, could I have made a difference? I thought of us boys lined up in the pews, waiting for our turn in the confessional. *Wudja do?* We'd been taught that God was mad at us and we were separated from him by our "sin." It broke my heart to think that my father might have felt the same way.

We buried my father just after Memorial Day. I spent that summer and fall playing golf every day, most days more than once—a morning round, lunch, then a round in the afternoon. I wasn't sure what else to do: my dad no longer needed me, the Archdiocese didn't want me, and someone else was running my newspaper. After about eight months on the links, it became clear I wasn't going to qualify for the Senior Tour even if I played every day for the next ten years. But golf filled a gap; it gave me a destination every morning. I was accustomed to getting up early and charging to the office, so I just started charging to the course instead. It challenged me for a time and gave me something to do. I played in the extreme heat, in the rain, in the dark; I even played most days through that winter, as I bought a cover for my cart, installed a propane heater, wore warm wool sweaters and kept a thermos of hot coffee close at hand. This sounds pretty good, even to me as I write about it almost ten years later, but it really was a case of too much of a good thing, and I soon began to find these days lacking in purpose and meaning. Don't get me wrong; I think once a person's life work is done, golf or fishing or any other recreational activity can be a healthy and joyous way to spend one's days, but on some level I knew I hadn't even *begun* my life's work. I couldn't verbalize this idea, and I certainly wouldn't admit I was feeling this way, but I knew. If I could only know what that work was—if I could get past the visceral instinct of The Deal and put some cement under the floor of the idea—I'd be more than happy to work as hard as I always had. I just didn't know what I was supposed to do.

FATHER KNOWS BEST?

Eventually, I did what I had always done: I began to see the slight from the Archdiocese as a meaningful event. Maybe God (or Whoever) didn't want me riding on a truck in my attempt to live up to my end of The Deal; maybe money wasn't the medium I should use to balance the books. What if my experience in Rome, my discovery, if you will, wasn't just pointing me toward my purpose—what if it *was* my purpose? It dawned on me that the sense of oneness I had experienced that night in my dorm room—the transcendent connection with something spiritual inside me—was the most important thing I had to offer. Maybe *that* was the real responsibility, not refrigerators. In this light, I could see the last 20 years of my life as a testimony to the incredible spiritual power each of us possesses once we recognize its Source. Maybe what God (or Whoever) really wanted me to do was tell my story.

I began to believe that this was the right time to write about The Deal. If I shared my testimony, I thought, The Deal could inspire others, especially young Catholics finding their way in the world. I had always thought that navigating life in our 20s was the most difficult part of the journey, so I would target a message of hope and encouragement to that group. I was still young myself, still cool enough to get their attention with my story. I thought my example could get younger people to focus early on the power of Spirit within themselves and help them overcome the obstacles, setbacks, and discouragement they were getting slammed with just as adult life was beginning.

I had been angry or disappointed with the Church in one way or another for most of my life. I was angrier than ever after what had happened in my father's hospital room. And yet I still considered myself a good Catholic. I still expected to find my direction and purpose within the context of the Church, and I still wanted the sanction of the institution as I went about repaying my debt. So I went to a local parish priest to ask for spiritual direction. He had recently been appointed pastor of the newest parish in the metro area after spending many years as a college chaplain, so I felt confident he would appreciate my wish to speak to younger people. More serendipity? Another perfectly positioned lifeline for me?

Father Will was charming and easy to talk to, but also very busy establishing his new parish, so he turned down my request for formal spiritual direction. But he did agree to meet with me. I liked him immediately and felt I could trust his judgment.

We met for lunch at J. Alexander's, a high-end eatery that was usually packed with heavyweights in power ties. The atmosphere provided a sense of privacy at our table underneath the din of deal-making all around. I was excited and a little nervous, not about eating at the power spot—I had eaten there regularly during my publishing days—but because in the 20 years since Rome, I had not told a single person about The Deal. I had kept it to myself all these years because I knew it would sound preposterous until there was tangible evidence. Father Will was going to be the first person to hear my story.

I felt like a kid on a first date or an applicant for an important job, rehearsing lines in my head. I was more than a little self-conscious about talking about The Deal for the first time, and I didn't know quite how to frame it in a way that wouldn't make me appear a little touched. After all, I was a pragmatic businessperson with a track record of being pretty well planted in reality. So I decided I'd take a businesslike stance. I had been a consultant, and I had hired consultants to help turn the *Daily News* around, so I would try to approach Father Will in the same way, as a professional who could advise me and be of service to me.

The conversation began with the usual small talk that goes with meeting someone new. Father Will told me about his background as a chaplain at several nearby universities. Now, he said, he was humbled by the challenge of building a new parish from scratch. "I understand, Father," I told him, trying to lay the groundwork for my pitch. "But I believe that life has a way of preparing a person for the work that will define their life."

After a bit more of this, he was ready to cut to the chase. "Enough about me, Tim, what is on your mind?"

"Well, Father, I—I want to write a book," I blurted. Just like that, no couching it like I'd planned.

"About what?"

"Well . . . sort of . . . well, you see, I think that people are leaving the Church . . . and I think that . . . well, I can sort of reach out to them . . . I mean I think I can reach a man's heart through his head." I was off to a terrible start. My plan to lead with my powerful story of the incident in Rome, followed by my very tangible success, went out the window as I reverted to my old habits of obsequiousness in the presence of a priest.

"So," Father Will prompted, "you want to write a book about theology?"

"Yeah, that's it, sort of about theology." What a babbling idiot I had become! That wasn't it at all. I felt my face get hot and I knew I was blushing. I was losing control of my intended delivery. Why was it so damned important for me to get his blessing anyway? I barely knew this guy. *Okay, try to start this over,* I said to myself.

"Father, here's the thing: I've recently sold my company and I've come into some money and I want to write about the way in which it unfolded. But I don't want to just write a story about another guy who made a lot of money; I want to tell the story that began years ago while studying theology in Rome. How I've perceived this to be a deal made with God and this result is just the first part of it." I was gaining a little stride now, a little confidence.

"You're saying God made you rich?" asked Father Will.

"Well, yes . . . but it isn't that simple."

"Tell me about it."

So I settled down and proceeded to tell him the story, from the night in Rome forward to that very day. I told him that I was positive of the Source of my success and I thought I should share my story as testament to this powerful spiritual connection I had made by writing a book about it aimed at people in the half-generation behind me. "I think my story can motivate young Catholics to stay in the Church," I explained, "and help them realize that the path to their success starts within it."

As soon as the words were out of my mouth, I wondered why I'd phrased it that way. To say that I wanted to encourage young people to stay in the Church—that wasn't exactly how I felt. Now that I had started to talk about it for the first time, the story began to take on a slightly different cast from what I had thought for all those years. I was starting, ever so slightly, to grasp that I might have made The Deal with something much larger than the Church. But I didn't tell that to Father Will. For some reason I wanted the Church to sanction The Deal and I needed Father Will's approval to seal it.

He seemed intrigued, but he wasn't exactly reacting with unbridled enthusiasm for my project. "What credentials do you have to write about this topic?" he asked.

"Credentials?"

"Yes. What advanced degree do you have?"

"Well, I don't actually have *any* degree," I explained. "I left college before I earned my degree. Why, Father, do you think that's important?"

"Yes, Tim, it *is* important. I think you should consider writing your story, but first you should go back to college and get at least your undergraduate degree and maybe even a master's before you expect to have any credibility with Catholic readers." He then proceeded to give me a little lecture about the importance of the "proper education," but I lost track after that point. I fell hard into my own head and the world was spinning. I was literally feeling dizzy and I couldn't really focus on what he was saying anymore. I nervously sipped my water instead.

After the lecture was over and his rebuke complete, I put up a timid rebuttal. I argued that my life was a tribute to a spiritual reality much larger than anything a degree would prove. But in reality I was demoralized, intimidated, and ultimately persuaded by his position. The glimpse of something larger faded.

When lunch was over, I was discouraged and embarrassed, the way I'd felt after meetings with priests for most of my life, except, of course, Father Tony back at Carmel. Who was I to think I had anything of value to say to the world? Many business associates and former clients had been encouraging me to write a book about my management principles and techniques, but I didn't want to—that could wait. I wanted to live up to my end of The Deal and if going back to school was what I had to do, then I would buck up and do it.

I listened inside. For the first time in many years, the voice was quiet, no intuition about whether or not I should listen to Father Will's advice. I didn't think I had a choice. Father knows best, right?

ADULT EDUCATION

So, about a year and a half out from selling the business, I went back to college. I enrolled at a small Catholic university about 90 minutes from my house to gain the credibility the priest thought I lacked. By this time, I had traded my BMW for a pickup truck and I enjoyed the long drive along scenic country roads to school and back. The plan was to complete the college degree I'd walked away from 20 years before. Theology had continued to be an intermittent topic of interest on my reading menu since I dropped out, so it wasn't difficult to reengage with the subject matter. I took two classes that semester, one about the Protestant Reformation and another on the New Testament.

I lasted until the day the professor went on a rant, claiming that wealth was evil, that every person with money had made a pact with the devil, on and on. He was stretching Bible quotes— Matthew 19:24, "It is easier for a camel to pass through the eye of a needle than for a rich man to enter the Kingdom of Heaven," was just the tip of the iceberg—to support his argument to these young, impressionable students, most of whom came from affluent homes. As much as I wanted to challenge this immature man, I realized that if I opened my mouth, I would begin a debate that would lead nowhere. I would have liked to defend the parents of the other, younger students, but I felt zero need to defend myself in face of such ignorant and misguided proclamations. In another setting, I would have happily taken the bait and gleefully engaged the professor, but I left that particular class with my tongue bleeding, never to return. I obeyed the voice inside that told me to be bigger than the small-minded professor; I knew I wasn't an evil rich guy and should not be goaded into defending my life. One thing was obvious—I was again out of place. So much for my return to academia.

I was batting a thousand. I couldn't get a job as a volunteer, I was terrible at golf and getting worse by the day, and if I continued hanging around a college campus I was probably going to assault some poor professor. So I decided to take the next logical step in an ongoing, albeit inadvertent, attempt to destroy my ego. I, the yuppie who had never even built a model airplane, would build a log cabin in the woods of Linn County, Kansas.

TIMBER HILL

After several attempts to realize the path I must take to complete The Deal, I was itching for work to fill my days and spend my abundant energy. I had been the happiest and most productive in my adult life when I was working the hardest. I wasn't comfortable being idle, and I didn't want my three kids to see me doing anything less than working hard to accomplish a goal. Several things coalesced to make my decision about what to do next. First, after being behind a desk for so many years, I wanted to pursue something outdoors. Second, I wanted to work with my hands for a change. Third, I wanted to do something different yet continue to use my life as an example of the power of setting a goal and believing in yourself to accomplish it. And lastly, I wanted to have a sanctuary for writing my story when I found the wisdom, the voice, and the point of view I was seeking. I still felt I had something important to say, but first I needed time to sort through the confusion and disillusionment of the last two years.

On my long drives to and from school, I'd been seduced by the country settings I passed through. I realized that the real attraction of golf for me was being outdoors traipsing over hill and dale, immersing myself in the beauty of flora and fauna. Then, after visiting an old farm that a friend had turned into a country retreat for hiking, hunting, and fishing, I decided I would create one of my own. I drew a circle on a map with a radius of about an hour's drive from our home and began shopping for land. Once I found the perfect piece of ground, I would commence my next big thing—I would create a piece of country heaven for my family and me.

I would build a log cabin with my own two hands. I would continue to set an example to my kids, I would spend ample time outdoors, and I would have the sanctuary to write. I was hoping the time alone in the woods would give me the time and solitude to gain clarity and perspective about my message. I was building a platform to hold up my end of The Deal.

For the next several years, I spent most of my time living in a small room in a metal barn an hour outside of town while I designed and built a log home perched atop a picturesque hill at the edge of the woods. I would come to call this slice of country heaven Timber Hill. The hard-charging, editorial-writing, self-professed greatest salesman in the world was in the woods playing with dangerous tools. I figured the rewards I had gotten emotion-ally—or spiritually—from building my company, I could get from building something with my hands as well. I got this and much more in the process.

That initial loss of identity from selling my company soon turned into an all-out assault on my rather sizable ego. I don't think a person could do what I had done in the business world without a pretty big ego, but I hadn't realized yet that mine was the dominant part of me. Ego is not a bad thing, just a part of being human, and like many aspects of human life, it ebbs and flows. I never set out to change it or eliminate it or bring it under control; but, like a pendulum, after I left my identity as "the boss" behind, my prodigious ego began to swing steadily in the opposite direction. I was changing, without intending to do so, the very idea of myself.

I created a new world for myself in which I didn't know any-thing. I had never lived in the country, I'd never built anything except businesses, and I'd never used power tools or heavy equipment or guns (all of which I would become surprisingly proficient with). I was trained to read financial statements and press releases, not blueprints and electrical schematics. The seemingly endless flow of external success and positive feedback from the world gave way to the deafening silence of self-doubt. In the business world, I won each day before it began through planning, preparation, and self-confidence. Now each day in the woods beat me up as I struggled to create something out of nothing with absolutely no experience in this new arena to give me confidence.

Maybe I had finally taken too big a bite, met a challenge bigger than me, run into an objective that would crush me. This new life was humbling—but it was exhilarating too. I loved working with my hands to accomplish a little something each day. My ego evaporated in the face of this new kind of work, but my confidence, a different kind of confidence this time, returned as my skill set changed. I was learning something new, and, as I'd discovered in the business world, people are happiest when learning. I was learning carpentry, hunting, planting, shooting, all new skills and all very exciting to a suburban yuppie who had always worn button-down shirts and Allen Edmonds shoes.

BANNED BOOKS

One thing I brought with me from my former life was a passion for reading and learning. But I found that now my interest wasn't in reading about business or anything else to do with success in the external world. I was once again asking questions about life, but this time the questions were not about "succeeding" in life or winning friends or influencing people or any of that. I was now more interested in what was going on inside me. What was happening to my ego? Where did it go? Why didn't I miss it? Was it coming back?

As was my custom, I began buying books about things I wanted to learn. This time however, perhaps because I was still angry— over the indifference of the Archdiocese, the discouraging advice of Father Will, the vitriol of the professor, plus the way the Church had let my dad down—I was going to loosen the chain a little bit. I had a habit of avoiding anything that didn't readily fit into my indoctrinated belief system. To put it another way, if it would offend the nuns, I didn't buy the book. All along I'd been looking *within* the Church to find the answers to the questions that had dogged me for most of my life; now it was time to step outside the box to seek the Truth I longed for.

As usual, I began by visiting my local bookstore to see what caught my eye. To celebrate my newfound liberation of the mind, I started with an author by the name of Joseph Girzone, a retired Catholic priest. (Come on, he was retired! I was making *some* progress, right?) I read his book *Joshua*, a sweet and lighthearted fictional tale about Jesus living in today's society. I would quickly read several others in his Joshua series and immensely enjoy each one. *Joshua and the City, Joshua and the Shepherd,* and *Joshua and the Children* touched me in their simple message, but they gave me a new way to think about Jesus as well. They got me to thinking about his human side in ways I never had before; they expanded my view of him and gave me permission to continue reading more about him. Reading fiction about Jesus before that would have felt improper in some way. Girzone, being a retired priest, played a big role in gently moving me toward exploring Jesus in ways that I would never had allowed before. What *would* Jesus do and say if he were here today? What would he think about the very questions I was having about Catholicism at that very moment and throughout my life?

Since I'd enjoyed this first foray into religious fiction, I next tried out the wildly popular and widely read *Left Behind,* the first book in a series that told a modern-day tale based on the Book of Revelation. The premise of the series is centered on a family group that survives the Rapture, which is a fundamentalist view of the End Times, a belief that God will take the faithful bodily up to Heaven in one moment while those left behind (including Catholics, in this story) will face the literal tribulations prophesied in the apocalyptic narrative of Revelation. I'd be lying if I said these books weren't page-turners, but the theology behind them was more than a little far-fetched for me. I've always had a problem with literal fundamentalism of any kind, so they did little to teach or inform me, but I did read eight in the series before I had my fill of their point of view.

Reading religious fiction was fun, but it wasn't moving me any closer to the evolved perspectives on religion that I was seeking. To gain information but stick with the idea of nontraditional viewpoints, I progressed to reading the Gnostic Gospels, alternate testimonies to the life and teaching of Jesus, documents that were banned from the canon of Christianity in the formative centuries of the faith. They were summarily destroyed over a thousand years ago, but portions of some have been rediscovered, some in 1898 and many more in 1945 in Nag Hammadi, Egypt.

I wanted to read these partly because I knew that as a Catholic I wasn't supposed to; these texts were taboo because they "contradicted" what the four canonical Gospels stated about Jesus' life and teaching. But mostly it was because, in spite of the doctrinal issues I'd had with Catholicism, I had always been interested in and attracted to stories about Jesus. The Gnostic Gospels are stories about Jesus told from a different perspective than the four in the Bible, and I wanted to see what they had to say. This was the beginning of a private religious revolution—as well as a much-needed spiritual evolution that gave me a stronger connection to my own inner knowingness, the "voice" within that I'd been listening to all those years.

THE KNOWINGNESS

The word *Gnostic* comes from the Greek word *gnosis,* which simply means "knowledge." As I delved into the Gnostic writings, I discovered that they pointed seekers of the Divine in a very different direction than the Church-approved teachings I knew. I read in the Gospel of Thomas: "If your leaders say to you, 'Look, the (Father's) kingdom is in the sky,' then the birds of the sky will precede you. If they say to you, 'It is in the sea,' then the fish will precede you. Rather, the kingdom is within you and it is outside you."[1] The Gospel of Mary Magdalene confirmed an instinct I had long had about the rule-bound Church of today, whose dogmas and doctrines had caused my father so much suffering: "I tell you that the Son of Man is within you all! Seek him inside; those who search diligently and earnestly shall surely find him. Then leave and preach the truth of the kingdom to those with ears to hear; don't invent rules beyond those I've given. Don't make laws like law-makers do."[2] And elsewhere, Thomas made a startling statement that seemed to put us all on a level with Jesus, if not with the Divine itself: "For God's Kingdom dwells in your heart and all around you; when you know yourself you too shall be known! You'll be aware that you're the sons and daughters of our living father."[3]

I felt as if the pieces were falling into place at last. The idea of experiencing God directly within oneself was consistent with my own life's experience. It seemed to confirm the same lurking suspicion I had had about spirituality since that momentous night in Rome, more than 20 years before I discovered these texts for myself. They seemed to ratify my lifelong reservations about dogma. That they had been banned and destroyed during the battles over Christian theology during the formative years of the Church increased the sense of "conspiracy" I had long harbored about the religion of my birth.

I was realizing that my own sense of knowingness was not in the least bit original—that the belief in an inner connection had been spoken of during the earliest years after Jesus, that maybe he had espoused it himself, as I had suspected all along. Followers of Jesus, it seemed, had taught and preached the very things I had experienced, and had their writings been part of my Christian indoctrination, I would have understood much sooner what had happened that night in Rome.

The relief was enormous, and it gave me new energy for my search. I didn't become a modern-day Gnostic or anything like that, but reading these texts made me hungry to read other material I had ignored throughout my life. I admitted how ignorant I really was about "religion" because of my blind attachment to Catholic theology, and the admission was freeing. I felt it was okay for me to become a "seeker." I was going to step out of the lifelong box of formal and dogmatic religion with an open mind and trust myself to not become too carried away in any one direction. I would no longer read only spiritual material endorsed by the Catholic Church—no more judging books by their covers.

Throughout my life, I'd been able to discern and assemble the necessary principles for worldly success by simply trusting what resonated within me, and I would do the same with this new topic of interest as well. When reading to enhance my business career, I came to rely on a physical feeling located somewhere in my solar plexus to tell me if I was reading something true or not. This is what I mean by "resonate." I always found a certain knowingness in the form of this physical vibration that guided me to apply only what would work, thereby eliminating a lot of trial and error (and making me look much smarter than I am). I concluded that the knowing guide I had had with me on my trek in the external world would be there to guide me to true principles in my internal life as well. If I read something about my spiritual development that conflicted with what my years of religious training taught me, I was going to go with the knowingness I felt existed within me—that trusty vibration in my solar plexus. Was this vibration *gnosis?*

The one thing I wouldn't do any longer was to fall into the dogmatic trap of a formal belief system—any belief system. I wasn't going to become a "church-hopper." I wasn't going to bounce from sect to sect looking for a place to belong; if formal religion turned out to be the answer, I was pretty sure Catholicism was the box that I fit into, but for now I wanted to explore outside the meta-box of formal religion entirely. Truth *must* be bigger than any one system offered.

When you have the time and quiet space that I had, you can really hear the truth resonate. I was learning to distinguish it. I stopped trying to find Truth in the religious belief system I was born into and started to inquire into my own spirituality instead. I was beginning, maybe for the first time, to seriously entertain the idea that there was more to God than a set of rules. And I wondered what had taken me so long—why I had allowed a giant institution to insert itself between me and the Spirit that I had known for years existed inside. Why had I been so reluctant to admit what I knew to be true?

Something had kept me tied to the Church even as more and more signs pointed the other way—maybe habit, maybe nostalgia, maybe fear. Or maybe—just maybe—there was a bigger reason. Maybe I *had* to keep trying and failing to consummate The Deal with the Church in order to realize that the Church wasn't the interested party. Maybe I *had* to fight my way to this essential personal freedom from it in order to fully understand what had happened that night in Rome and articulate it in a meaningful way to others.

How could I ever get to know the Spirit that lived inside me by turning to an impersonal, institutional liaison, one that only knew I existed by the deposits I made in the collection basket? The Church seemed so external, so ritualistic. I was not interested in externals or rituals. I wanted Truth. I believed Jesus when he said, "You shall know the truth and it will set you free." In that view—as in all my experience—knowing was something that came from within. He didn't say I would learn the Truth, or be taught the Truth, Jesus said I would *know* the Truth. I began to realize what this Truth could free me from—and to get excited about just what it might free me *for*.

THE WALDEN YEARS

My vision of a small cabin in the woods had expanded into a beautiful log home sitting majestically on top of the highest ridge in the county, overlooking more than a hundred acres of fields and perched on the timberline of about a hundred more acres of beautiful hardwood. While I built the house, I lived a spartan life in a newly built metal barn with my books and my dog Blue. I traveled back to our home in town every Friday evening to spend the weekend with my family and returned on Monday morning to my building project and my books.

My year in "Walden Woods" turned into almost seven.

I was finding more and more satisfaction and connection through my reading, discovering my own deeply rooted and very personal spirituality beneath a mass of unnecessary book learning about religion. This mass was like a tumor pressing on a vital organ, and it wasn't easy to remove. Eight years of grade school (nuns), four years of high school (priests and brothers), and three years of college (Jesuits), capped by a climactic year of studying in Rome (more Jesuits)—after all that, I finally understood that "religion" wasn't working in sync with my own knowingness about the Spirit within me. Instead of teaching me to embrace this knowingness, my training had taught me to trust religion and distrust myself when it came to spiritual truth. It was shocking, but somehow wondrously liberating, to uncover the hold that religion had on my life.

I continued to read what I wanted to read and interpret it for myself. (Egad!) When it resonated, I trusted that my own knowingness was showing me Truth. I tried to forget all of the imposed interpretations I had been raised with. I let the understanding become fresh and personal. (Egad again!) The vibration in my solar plexus was active and I began to understand it as simply a "gut feeling."

All of those years, the knowingness I'd felt at critical junctures of life was the "voice" of God guiding me. Now I was sensing a deepening relationship with God, but at the same time coming to understand that "God" was just a word, just a name for an entity that was becoming more and more personally available to me. I wasn't using ritual or relying on a third-party institution to be the go-between between "God" and me. I approached Him directly and I found Him patiently waiting inside of me.

I had always believed that I was made up of part flesh and part "something else." I realized, when I bypassed the rituals, that the "something else" was a direct link to the Universal Intelligence that religion calls God. This link, this Spirit, was not something that needed to be awakened (it had never been asleep), just affirmed and acknowledged in a new way. Finally, after years spent stuck in a system of belief that did not and could not evolve, my mind was evolving to connect to the One Universal Mind behind all that is.

I came to the conclusion that organized, doctrinal religion— and specifically, from my point of view, Catholicism—if adhered to unthinkingly and never questioned, has the power to *keep* an individual from knowing God. *Knowing religion is not knowing God.* Religion maintains the myth of duality by its very nature; it can be no other way. Most religious systems are *transactional,* when in fact their founders were not engaged in transactions—they were *transformed* by their own experience, which they tried to share.

For me, religion was always about adherence to a set of behaviors and beliefs and not so much about finding the Truth of God, which is what my spirit most desired to know. I looked to religion to show me how to unleash the unlimited power of Infinite Intelligence in my life, and religion taught me to turn to *religion* for all of my needs. I wanted to align myself with that power, but religion wanted me to align myself with *it.*

I guess this never resonated with me, hence the life of searching.

It took those years in the woods for me to find the time to search on my own and the right place to look. I know many people are provoked into seeking spiritual truth by something that makes them question their assumptions and their priorities. A traumatic loss of some sort or some catastrophic life event shakes their world so deeply it changes them forever. I'm fortunate to have been given the great opportunity to pursue my quest from a very safe and comfortable time in my life.

I've spent the better part of the last decade attempting to square up the corners of my own beliefs. I've questioned *everything* I was taught, and in the process, I've drawn some new conclusions. I've gained a new understanding of religion and spirituality. I can see how flawed some of my old beliefs were. The scariest question for me now is: what would have become of my spiritual life had I not been blessed with the opportunity to step out of the action for a while? What about all those who never get a chance for that kind of extended reflection and contemplation? I hope that this book finds its way into their hands and that my experience offers them a shortcut I never found.

What you're reading in this book is what I have contemplated. It's what I know at this time in my life. In some areas I'm certain of my understanding, in most areas I'm still evolving, and in some I just don't know yet. I suspect that if I write about the same topics ten years from now, the things I *know* will have evolved.

Here's what I think I know as I leave the "Walden Years" of my life:

- My ego is like a pendulum. It swings from controlling me to nearly disappearing, depending on what I need from it to move through my human experience.

- All those years ago in Rome, I made The Deal with something much larger than the institutional Catholic Church. It just took me 20 years to figure out what.

- Being trapped in a doctrinal belief system kept me from forging a personal connection to the Universal Mind that had been reaching out to me for most of my life.

- Truth resonates if you let it.

- Religion and spirituality are not the same thing. They may or may not be mutually exclusive. Some people may find spirituality in the dogma of formal religion—I do not.

- My responsibility to The Deal wasn't to be a Church apologist or keep young Catholics in the fold or anything like that. It was to ask the questions that would lead me to my own understanding of Truth—and maybe to shine a small light on the path for any who come after me on the same quest.

- I don't feel guilty about my connection to God sans dogma. I love it!

FOURTEEN

PRACTICING ONENESS

The Conversation of Our Life

Why am I here? What is my purpose? Where am I going? Our innate impulse to seek out answers to these primal questions—our impulse to *know*—is what lifts us above the rest of creation and defines us as human beings. As a species, we naturally quest for knowledge about reality (truth); as individual men and women, we ask fundamental questions about the meaning of our own lives (purpose). These fundamental questions give rise to our Ascending Urge and are as old as humanity itself.

To whom are we speaking when we ask these questions? They *must* be intended for a higher power; who could answer such questions but intelligence beyond our own? Individualized intelligence (man) seeks answers of Universal Intelligence (God). The questions are as personal as can be—yet rational human minds the world over have put them in an institutional context by setting up organized religions to guide us to the answers.

Does the worldwide response of religion satisfy this common urge of the human spirit? That particular question is too big for me to answer; maybe it does, maybe it doesn't. Who knows for sure?

But our aim at this point is not to evaluate mankind's collective connection to God. Our focus is much more narrow; it's empirical and individual. And the question of our Ascending Urge, as global as it seems to be, in the end is a very personal question.

For myself, I can say that religion, at least the formalized, doctrinized variety, got in the way of my own Ascending Urge. My indoctrination took such deep root that I was unable for many years to understand the very personal way in which God was touching me. It was not until I really began to allow my *experience* with Spirit to override my theoretical and theological *understanding* of it that I began to come closer to the truth about my own journey. Only when I acknowledged the knowingness inside for what it really was, and *stopped trying to frame my experience with doctrine,* did I learn to trust the more personal truth of this intimate relationship.

I realize that the idea of a direct and completely *personal* relationship with God can't be taught on a massive scale—it's bad for business (Church business, that is) and weakens the structure of the institution. But I have come to understand that the Ascending Urge isn't seeking structure as much as it is craving connection. As universal as the urge is, it becomes an intensely intimate affair between each person and his or her individual indwelling of God: because it is from *inside us* that the call emanates, *inside us* is where we must respond. In effect, our Ascending Urge is the voice of God attempting to begin the conversation of our life.

How do we enter this conversation, then? How do we open a channel of communication with the Divine? Even if we discern, as I did, the "voice of God" speaking to us in the form of our own intuition or innate knowing, we need a way to make our own voices heard. Maybe the real question that man's Ascending Urge asks is: "How do I pray?"

When we start to think about the practice (*not* the belief system) of addressing ourselves to God, we have no shortage of questions.

Where, when, and how should we pray?

What did Jesus say about praying?

Can we affect the will of God through prayer?

Does God respond to one person's prayers and ignore another's?

Do we give up our free will when we seek God's intercession?

Do we need religion to pray?

Of course, all of these questions are just different ways to ask the biggest, most basic question of all. *Hello, is anybody in there?*

WHAT IS PRAYER?

Prayer is the act of communicating with a deity or spirit for one of several reasons: petitioning for help, giving thanks, confessing sin, or asking for guidance, to name the most common. The word *prayer* comes from the Latin verb *precari*, which means "to beg." The traditional Christian definition of prayer is "the raising of one's mind and heart to God or requesting of good things from God."[1] Many people would describe prayer as simply "talking to God."

Prayer means different things to different people, from the child's melodious bedtime recital—*I pray the Lord my soul to take*—to the repetition of the Rosary, the rise and fall of Gregorian chant, the quietude of the mind in meditation, the contemplation of nature, or the ritual steps of an aboriginal dance. Nearly all of the world's major religions espouse prayer in some form, some highly ritualized, some more spontaneous and open. Though there seems to be a universal *call* to prayer, there is no universal interpretation of it.

But all of these forms of prayer have something in common: they are all *practices*. They all take a person past belief and into action, no matter how passive the action may seem.

Religion without prayer, made up solely of beliefs, doesn't work because it does not include the action—the practice—that brings the adherent in touch with God. *Religion without prayer* is just a collection of doctrines. On the other hand, *prayer without religion* is entirely possible; one can commune with the Universal Spirit without knowing anything about doctrine.

Prayer can be formal or spontaneous; it can be designated to a special time and place or it can permeate every waking moment. It may be a 24/7 undertaking or a special time set aside. To some it is a discreet activity conducted in private, to others it is a public display. For some, prayer requires movement like dance or gesture; for others it calls for complete stillness of the body and silence of the mind. Prayer is an attitude; it is mental *and* spiritual.

Man speaks to God via prayer and God speaks back to man via the channels of the human heart in the form of intuition, insight, inspiration, or revelation. Spirit speaks to us when we create. It is speaking to me as I write this, and maybe it is speaking to you as you read it.

THE SECRET ROOM

"And when you pray do not imitate the hypocrites: they love to say their prayers standing up in the synagogues and at the street corners for people to see them. I tell you most solemnly, they have had their reward. But when you pray, go to your private room and when you have shut your door, pray to your Father who is in that secret place, and your Father who sees all that is done in secret will reward you."[2]

Jesus' instructions to his disciples on the proper practice of prayer are clear. He is suggesting that the place to find God is inside yourself—that when you approach Him there, within that most secret of places, your own heart, he will reward you. The reward of the hypocrites is merely the attention they call to themselves by making a public spectacle of their prayer.

But many religious belief systems teach adherents to pray to a remote being. We are taught to pray in a church, temple, mosque, or synagogue—in "God's house," not our "secret place." We are taught to couch our prayers in certain terms and to look upon statues, icons, and pictures as we pray. Even the most often prayed of all Christian prayers begins: *Our Father, who art in Heaven . . .* Unless and until we accept that Jesus was showing us the "Kingdom of Heaven" within each of our hearts individually, this prayer places us from the outset in a posture of duality, of separation from God. We are here on earth and He "art in Heaven." And from a position of separation, we assume the posture of having to convince God that our prayer is worthy, which is really a position of doubt. One needs to catch God in the right mood or make the right argument to persuade Him.

It is difficult to believe in a God who favors one person over another. It is difficult to believe that God could be in a mood to listen to us one day and ignore us the next day. God doesn't have moods or tendencies, *we do.* God doesn't have a more favorable opinion of one over another, *we only fear that He does.* God is predisposed to love His creation—*all of it, all of the time.* We are the ones who create the illusion of a fickle God by our doubt. So the act of praying has absolutely no effect on the will of God; it only affects us, the ones doing the praying, by giving the assurance that He and we are of the same mind. Our own unity with Him, not our ability to influence Him, manifests the results in our lives that we desire. As Eric Butterworth puts it, "Prayer is not something we do to God but to ourselves."[3]

In the Gospel of John, Jesus instructs, "God is spirit, and those who worship must worship in spirit and truth."[4] God "responds" to all who think according to His true essence. Think of each person as a "cup of God." If you were to take a cup of water from the ocean, it would have all of the properties of the ocean. Of course, it would not have the volume of the ocean, but the properties would be identical. Within this cup of ocean water you would find the ocean itself. When you put the cup of water back into the ocean, at once it would come into full unity with the ocean again with no separation whatsoever. The same is true of mankind. We are "cups" of consciousness derived of the Universal Consciousness that is God. Our properties are identical to God; we are just finite vessels and He is Infinite Source.

When we pray with a sense of this true relationship (spirit and truth), we are part of God and He is part of us. There is no separation, so we are no longer praying upward or outward; we are praying inward to where we can be certain we are heard. We can also be certain that God's "mood" or "disposition" is not a factor. (Our mood and disposition, however, are an entirely different matter. If we hold doubt, uncertainty, or separation in our hearts as we pray, it may feel like God is not listening.)

We can be sure our best interest *is* the interest of God. We can trust the voice of God as heard through intuition, that "gut feeling" we all experience, without question. *We need not overcome God's reluctance to help us, we need only accept His readiness to do so.*

Our fear of God is the result of the duality we are taught. We fear we are *not worthy* of God's attention because we've been taught that we are not worthy *to receive* him. We fear that our offenses are too great, that we've lost our right to ask for His help and guidance, because we are taught that He sits in judgment and punishes. But the fear itself is the barrier between us and what God intends for us. *Fear is the opposite of faith.*

When we realize what Jesus really meant about the Kingdom of Heaven, we get a new perspective. If the simple premise that he taught us means that the kingdom is found in our own hearts, everything changes. Duality dissolves in the reality of oneness.

I was *engaging* God when I traveled through the night on my way home from Texas as a lost teenager, I *experienced* God that momentous night in Rome, and God was *guiding* me through my career, but it took a long time of contemplation and stillness in the woods to realize that I had been ignoring my oneness with God in favor of the duality I was taught. When I made this distinction, my entire history began to make more sense, and so did my purpose for the future.

In some ways, my life had been a continual prayer, an ongoing conversation with God—but much of that time I'd been looking outward and upward, while all the while my inner knowingness was comfortably "praying" without my conscious awareness. Sometimes the conversation is taking place whether we know it or not.

FREE WILL AND PRAYER

The Catechism states that we do not initiate conversations with God: "In prayer, God's initiative of love always comes first; our own first step is always a response. As God gradually reveals himself, prayer appears as a reciprocal call, a covenant drama."[5] Jesus underlines God's omniscience with the idea that our prayers are answered before we pray them: "In your prayers do not babble as the pagans do, for they think that by using many words they will make themselves heard. Do not pray like them; your Father knows what you need before you ask him."[6] Some use these statements to argue that the free will of mankind is not that free after all. If God knows what we are going to pray and answers us, are we really free?

If God already knows what we need before we ask, then perhaps everything—even what we ask for—is predetermined and we have little to say about the course of our life. And if we are not initiating dialogue with God but always responding to His initiative, then our needs, and the fulfilling of them, are not in our control; we are merely puppets. But we are *not* puppets in a play directed by God; we are "co-conspirators" with God. Our individual intelligence accesses the Infinite Mind to manifest the outcomes in our life. The notion that God knows all we need before we do simply refers to the Knowingness that God is; it shows that we are constantly expanding toward God.

Of course, any knowledge we have is knowledge God already has too. So, when we realize a need and ask God to assist us in meeting it, we are expanding into the awareness that He is. By the time we articulate our desire in prayer, our knowingness (small k), or (individual) intuitive mind, has already connected with Knowingness (big K), or the One (Universal) Mind, to identify our need; our conscious human awareness is just catching up.

Without oneness with God, there is no prayer, just a lopsided, pleading monologue. It is when we achieve oneness that God transforms our life. This is the energy field, the quantum aspect of manifesting, that the much-discussed law of attraction touts. But it isn't our mental energy alone that powers this law; *it is our mental energy aligned with the will and intention of the Higher Power residing within us.* All manifestation begins with thought. Proper thought, centered on God, produces "miraculous" results; thought that doesn't include God produces the problems in our life.

In times of great strife in the world, fear runs amok, and this serves to reduce God's influence, not increase it. Faith is the medium in which the will of God has the greatest effect. If God existed *outside* His creation, this would not be the case. But the Creator is alive within all He creates, and the inner separation created by fear of lack is precisely what creates the lack.

BARTERING WITH GOD

"Ask, and it will be given to you; search, and you will find; knock, and the door will be opened to you. For the one who asks always receives; the one who searches always finds; the one who knocks always has the door opened for him. What father among you would hand his son a stone when he asked for bread? Or hand him a snake instead of a fish? Or hand him a scorpion if he asked for an egg?"[7]

Jesus' message here is very clear. God gives us what we ask for. There is no bartering, posturing, or trying to manipulate God— just ask and God gives, as we would give to one of our own.

We must move beyond the idea that a relationship with Spirit is transactional—that we must "do" in order to "get." The theology of transaction prevents us from entering into the truly transformational experience that communing with God can be. *We can never do, say, or pray anything that will influence the will of God.* However, we *can* align ourselves with the power that God wishes to give us that will transform us and let us grow in the direction of our desires. Prayer need not become ritualized; it must not be relegated to "professional" holy men or reduced to reading from a book or marginalized by performing a recital. It must take shape in the mind and heart of each person through an individual, ongoing conversation with the Spirit that powers each of us.

Jesus prayed often during his life. After he was baptized, as he prepared to begin his ministry, he spent 40 days in the wilderness, mostly praying. The night before he was taken into custody, he prayed. During his most compelling and most highly organized group lesson, the Sermon on the Mount, he even gave his followers a course in how to pray when he imparted the Lord's Prayer, which is the most common prayer among Christians to this day.

OUR FATHER, WHO ART INSIDE US

Jesus taught his disciples to pray because they had asked him how to do it. Much more than a ritualized recital, the Lord's Prayer—also known as the Our Father—is a formula for prayer as well as a prayer in itself. When we understand it correctly, it lays the groundwork for oneness and it shows us how to prepare our hearts and minds to commune with God. Nearly every intention the prayer communicates (there are seven) is in the affirmative. Jesus is not teaching us to beg God; he is teaching us to be in position to *accept* what we are *expecting* to happen.

In order for us to learn as Jesus intended, we must be mindful of his theology of the Kingdom of Heaven. When he talks about the Kingdom, we must remember he is pointing us inward. The Kingdom he means is not some place, mythical or physical, "up there" in Heaven; it is the real and physical space inside our very body. It is "in here," not "up there." We must start to look in the right place if we are to find God alive in our life, responding to our prayer.

Let's try it with the Lord's Prayer. Let's examine the words of this famous prayer, keeping in mind where the Kingdom is. Assume you are addressing God in "spirit and truth" as Jesus advises. Assume that the Kingdom of which he speaks is *internal and spiritual*—the Kingdom inside is where God dwells.

Our Father, who art in Heaven. When you say "who art in Heaven," think *who art inside me.* Immediately the prayer feels different, and it is the feeling of a prayer that is paramount, not the words. If Heaven is inside, then Jesus states this at the outset. "Our Father, who lives inside me . . ."

Hallowed be Thy name, Thy kingdom come. *Hallowed* means sacred, consecrated, sanctified. If the Kingdom is inside, and the one who resides there is the Holy One, then what does this say about the residence where he dwells? That it too is sanctified. Anywhere God lives is considered hallowed or sacred, and God lives within you, in "the Kingdom," in a divine dwelling. "Thy Kingdom come," following our paradigm of oneness, states that our Kingdom *has already* come, not *shall* come, to us. It is already here.

Thy will be done on earth as it is in Heaven. What is willed in Heaven, *this Kingdom inside,* is manifest on earth, or in the natural world. Jesus is stating that what is willed within us is produced without. Pop culture today discusses the law of attraction as a sort of photocopy machine, whereby whatever we think about creates an energy field in the world and the world automatically manifests exactly the energy we emit. Here, though, is the true law of attraction: whatever is willed in this place called Heaven, God's Kingdom inside, is manifest on earth.

Give us this day our daily bread. Today, God gives what we need. Our "daily bread" is whatever needs we have. Today. There is no mention of quantity or limit, no minimum daily requirement or maximum allowance, just the affirmative statement that our individual needs are fulfilled and we are sustained. Notice, also, that this is more of a command than a request. We needn't beg God for our "daily bread"; we only need to accept it. Jesus didn't say, "I beseech thee" or "I beg thee"; he stated, "Give."

And forgive us our trespasses, as we forgive those who trespass against us. God will forgive our human tendencies in proportion to our willingness to do the same for other humans. "Forgive us . . . as we forgive" means we will receive compassion commensurate with the compassion we give—but here again, we are initiating from a position *inside* how we will be dealt with *outside*. This illuminates Jesus' command to us, "Love thy neighbor," with a new light. Forgiveness is an act of love, perhaps the ultimate act of love. It doesn't unnecessarily flatter God by professing our love for Him; it states that we will show compassion to his creation by forgiving any who "trespass" against us. Jesus instructs us to love our enemy, an important point in our compact with God. We are instructing God—once again, not asking or begging Him—to forgive us in a measure equal to our forgiveness of others.

And lead us not into temptation, but deliver us from evil. This is distinctly another command and not a request. We are commanding that we be delivered from bad things in the world (evil) by our own volition via the One who resides within us. Our own heart allows us to succumb to temptation—never does God "lead" us there—so whom could this command be intended for? God wouldn't lead us into temptation, our humanity would, but God can certainly deliver us to a better place, away from the "evil" in the world. We are commanding our divine or spiritual self to protect us from our humanity.

If we direct this prayer inward and not out to some remote location, the answer is certain. *The Lord's Prayer* is more of a formula than a recipe. It shows us how to pray, not only what to say when we do pray. In prayer, we are not trying to knead God's will. We are stating in no uncertain terms, with no transparent attempt at manipulating Him, that we are commanding a result—and, more importantly, that we are willing to accept what we command.

Jesus of Nazareth, the enlightened carpenter, preached a Kingdom of Heaven, and he taught his followers to look within themselves to find it. But somewhere along the way, Jesus was made into God, and the world's largest religion exists today largely to worship him. The simple message Jesus brought is overshadowed by volumes and volumes of doctrine that justify the Church's authority and deify this special man, forgetting that he told us we were just like him.

Christians are taught that Jesus is The Christ, a concept that comes with many complicated mysteries attached. But Jesus himself taught about the Christ in us *all*, which is much less complicated. Conventional Christian principles of piety, frozen in the forms of antiquity, keep us gazing outward, addressing ourselves across a great distance to some remote entity we must manipulate or appease. But there is nothing remote about the Spirit that lives within, and the more we look outward, the farther from God we get.

Jesus taught us to pray to *Our Father*, who resides in the Kingdom of Heaven within us. The Buddha taught us to meditate until we discover the pure and awakened self beyond our human attachments—also within. Hindu saints taught us yoga, a physical practice that brings us to oneness with the Divine Essence of all being. The shaman taught us to walk with one foot in this world and the other in an inner world. The native spiritual masters taught us to dance as a way to a personal connection with nature, where Spirit permeates. Every belief system teaches us a practice to take us *beyond* belief and into an experience of the Divine. We can study doctrine and memorize dogma our whole life long and not make the slightest dent, but a proper posture in the practice of prayer—praying "in spirit and truth," engaging God whole-heartedly in the conversation of our life—can transform that life immediately. Instantaneously. Miraculously.

EPILOGUE

After I finished writing this book, I heard the familiar "voice" that my life had taught me never to ignore. I was ready for a break and I might have even secretly felt like rewarding myself for finally taking a meaningful stride toward balancing the books on The Deal. So when the trusty intuition that had been my guide for so long told me to go back to Rome, I didn't overthink it—I began to plan the trip. I was about to take the initiative of making my private quest public, and it made sense on many levels that Rome would be the place to find the equanimity and confidence to make such a brazen leap. My first trip to the Eternal City had been motivated by questions; this time it would be to seek ratification of some answers.

So in the fall of 2009, exactly 30 years after I'd arrived solo, sweating in my three-piece suit, to the unnerving reception of machine guns, I returned to Rome a little more poised, this time accompanied by my 27-year-old daughter, Kelly. I knew she was the perfect travel companion for this journey of rediscovery. She has the same inquisitive mind as her dad, and she'd be as enthusiastic as I was about ancient ruins, old churches, museums, and fine cuisine. I was delighted that "Beans" was excited to join me, and she was patient and understanding as I nervously shared, in bits and pieces, the ambiguous and enigmatic sanction I hoped to find by returning to Rome.

I was a bit chagrined to find that I wasn't as proficient a chaperone as I'd bragged I'd be. It's a good thing Beans grabbed a map from the concierge that first afternoon because I was quite irritated that they had moved the Coliseum since I'd last been in Rome. From my initial perspective, they had moved *everything*, and I needed to rely on her silly map to guide our tour for the first couple of days. But when I changed the perspective by renting a Vespa, the layout and the rhythm of the city came back in a flood of familiarity. We visited all the obligatory Roman sites—the Forum, Saint Peter's, the Via Veneto, dozens of churches, and all the famous fountains. We ate (and ate and ate some more!) in the Piazza Navona, dined out several times in Trastevere, found some cool off-the-beaten-path ristoranti, and took a shopping junket to Florence. We made friends with the staff at a café near our hotel where we relaxed after a long day touring and fueled up on cappuccino every morning.

Aside from an increased population of tourists (and McDonald's!), Rome hadn't changed much in 30 years. It was great to be back in one of my favorite cities with one of my favorite people. While strolling the halls of the Vatican Museum I marveled at the look on Kelly's face and took dozens of pictures of her taking pictures. I was happy and proud. But there was something I still had to do to make this journey complete.

One morning, after a late night of delightful dining in Trastevere, I left Kelly at the hotel to sleep late, hopped on the Vespa, and navigated my way to the top of Monte Mario. I motored up to the John Felice Rome Center and took off my helmet, sweating in the late September sun and was startled to see a ten-foot security gate blocking the once-open entryway to the picturesque little campus. The barrier was one of the few signs of the times I'd noticed in Rome but I was relieved, if a little saddened, to know that the current students were protected in ways we hadn't needed in 1979. When I rang the bell, the voice that answered sounded just like Vito, who had manned the desk 30 years before. In fact, it was Vito's nephew, and when I explained who I was, he buzzed me in, checked my passport, and invited me to stay as long as I liked.

The echoey halls with their marble floors were cool and refreshing after my sweaty journey. I walked to the cafeteria just as lunch was beginning and swiped a moon rock, *a staple of backpack fare.* Briefly, I was tempted to offer *an auditory accolade—wait, don't be a clod.*

I peeked into some of my old classrooms and could see the teachers in front of the class—*happy to be in Rome, without the seriousness most professors seemed to have back in the States.* It didn't seem appropriate to go into the dorm area, so I settled for snapping some pictures of my old room from the walkway behind the building. A pair of faded blue jeans hung from my balcony. *Could they . . . no, of course they couldn't.*

Out in the courtyard, I watched students congregating, acting like kids are supposed to act—*there were plenty of goofs to go around.* I ran into the wife of Renaldo, who still ran the snack bar in the basement, and chatted with her *speaking my own hybrid language—I called it Spantalian.* Renaldo was out, but she was sure he would remember me. I doubted it, until I recalled the night we goofs of old constructed a five-foot-high pyramid of empty Heineken cans. *How could he forget that?*

I meandered to *the red clay tennis court behind the school* to shoot a few baskets, only to discover it had been blacktopped.

So, something had changed after all. But when I made my way back into the convent building and walked down the basement hallway toward the old round chapel, everything felt the same again. I realized I was zeroing in on the real destination of this Roman holiday.

The quiet darkness became a sanctuary for reflection. I slipped in and took a seat in my familiar spot—in the back pew, the same one I'd occupied at daily Mass for two semesters. I took a few deep breaths and closed my eyes, and then, from that familiar perch, *I started to see the view of my life take shape . . .*

I felt a force of Spirit take hold of me with an incredible and unexplainable sense of oneness. Suddenly I understood with certainty that a person could come to communion with God from within. In a rush of overwhelming understanding, I knew the Church was a manmade institution that could not deliver a man to where God really dwelt.

Had I done justice to that instant of understanding in the 30 years since? Had I conducted my "investigation" into the religion of my birth as fairly as I could? Did I ask enough questions? Did I ask the *right* questions? Why had it taken me 30 years of inquiry to authenticate the flash of insight I'd had that night in my dorm room when God delivered the terms of The Deal?

Reflecting from the back pew, I figured out that asking questions wasn't a necessary means to a once-and-for-all end—it had become the essential, ongoing activity of a deepening awareness of Truth. It had taken 30 years of asking questions just to *begin* to make sense of an experience that changed the course of my life. Questions, I admitted, had actually become the cornerstone of my spiritual practice, and I acknowledged, with a sense of humor and a dose of humility, that I would keep asking them for as long as I live.

Questions. Beautiful, fantastic, enlightening, and exciting! Questions.

It has taken a long time and a lot of questions to complete my end run around dogma, but I'm now free from blind allegiance to a belief system *about* Jesus and liberated to actually gain more from the wisdom *of* Jesus. Stepping outside the box of formal religion, and eliminating the label affixed to it, has given me the freedom to investigate, explore, and even compare other strains of spiritual wisdom and thought—and every time I've done so, I have bolstered my understanding and appreciation of what Jesus tried to teach us. By following the trail to where my questions lead, I've come to understand his wisdom truly *is* universal. It points in the same direction that the wisdom of nearly all spiritual masters points: *inside.*

Most formal religions stopped asking questions around the time they transferred their deposits of faith to paper and this transference prevented them from evolving along with the ever-evolving human capacity to understand. For some people, formal religion *does* fulfill the internal impulse to connect with the Divine, but for an increasing number of men and women, the belief systems of yore no longer satisfy the Ascending Urge of an ever more expansive, more discerning mind.

So what does that mean for those who have not found the promise of religion fulfilled? For some, it's a lifetime of unsatisfied seeking; for some, a duty-bound adherence to rules and rituals that have lost their meaning; for others, a wholesale rejection of God. But those who can dispense with the formality of ritual, who can look past the deposits of dogma to the *wisdom* of the original depositor, become more likely to find a viable and vital personal connection to Truth. This requires asking questions— lots of questions—about what you were taught to believe and what you thought you believed.

I'm not trying to talk you into leaving your religion, nor am I trying to convince you to return to a religion you've left. What I *am* suggesting is that you ask the questions—and then listen for answers. You will know the Truth because it resonates loudly and clearly. You don't have to look "up there"; you can learn to look "in here," where, according to Jesus himself, the Kingdom of Heaven is. If you listen, you can't miss it.

Belief is not an end in itself. Belief is not the destination or purpose of religion. Belief is not the culmination of a transaction but the starting point of a transformation. Belief can lead to a deeper faith in the Divine, and this faith organically expresses itself in practice. Spiritual practice completes the transformation by opening the door to direct experience.

And once you *experience* God, nothing is ever the same again.

ACKNOWLEDGMENTS

It is often said that writing is a solitary, lonely experience. For me, writing is a solo endeavor to be sure, but it is rarely lonely.

But publishing? This is where the individual joins the team, where the soloist fuses with the symphony, where the lone wolf unites with the pack. And boy, was I was blessed with an incredible symphony of professionals who coordinated to give birth to the book you're now holding. For much of my adult life I've been putting ink on paper, but I'm as proud of what this team has produced as anything I've been associated with; I'm lucky to consort with the pros who made this happen.

First, I'd like to thank Anne Barthel, my insightful, amazingly intuitive, and wickedly cool editor. Editing, of course, is improving the writer's syntax, structure, and sentence formation, but it is so much more when done well. Anne's uncanny ability to navigate my mind allowed her to go well beyond fixing my word problems and absolving my numerous sins of syntax; she grasped the potential of this book better than I had conceived at the start. Our collaborative effort turned into a relationship that has benefited me much more than the professional editing she gave to this project. She is a mentor, a writing guru, a pretty damn good shrink, and most importantly a cherished friend. Thanks, Anne, for putting up with my intensity, passion, and schizophrenia—*I couldn't have done this without you.*

To Patricia Spadaro—a *real* coach. I thank you for believing in the vision of this project and for keeping the team focused on priorities. Your encouragement and unwavering support was a source of great inspiration. You understand the process of writing and of giving birth to a book, and your enthusiasm for doing things the right way was a lighthouse that guided me through the unknown waters of getting a book ready to publish. I thank you for always demanding my best and not giving me a pass when you knew I could do better—*you were always right.*

To Nigel Yorwerth—if Patricia is the lighthouse, you are the powerhouse. Your mastery of the publishing world brought this book to market. You're the quarterback who always called the right plays and the lens that somehow always kept the big picture in focus. Your leadership was invaluable—*I can't wait for our next project together.*

Thanks to Nita Ybarra for an elegant and powerful cover design, to Alan Barnett for the page design, and to Karin Bilich for designing a website and blog even I can handle. (Check it out at AViewFromTheBackPew.com.)

To my kids, Kelly, Tim, and Taylor, for never complaining while your dad disappeared into the woods during his search for Truth. The time I spent on Timber Hill would not have been possible had you not been as trouble-free as you've been. You, more than anyone, allowed me the freedom to search. My only regret is my frequent separation from you. Thanks for being a source of strength and pride and for holding me accountable—*you are the true blessings of my existence in this world.*

To Lynn, my wife and my best friend—thanks for always believing in my unconventional approach to life. Having a partner who swims against the flow must be difficult. You've never tried to steer me to the mainstream and you've been my biggest supporter and cheerleader. *With you the good times are always better and the bad times are only an illusion.*

To my mom, my dad, my grandmother, and my three brothers. Thanks for shaping the foundation of a wonderful life. *Dad, I miss you.*

Thanks to my friends who encouraged me to write this book and who remained even when I got lost in the process.

To the Higher Power that guides my life—I'm grateful to have you riding shotgun. Anyone who has given birth to a creative project understands there is a moment in each creative session where the process goes beyond the capacity of your own mind; you accept and welcome the help that comes from beyond the borders of your self and marvel at the collaboration with something more than you. If I hadn't submitted to this power, this book would still be a dream. Once I gave into the fact that I wasn't going to write this book alone, it wrote itself.

To the readers of this book: In the end, this effort is most essentially dedicated to you. I applaud your courage to question and your dedication to seek answers. I know my conclusions may vary from yours and I hope yours may help shed new light on mine. I thank you for the trust you've placed in me, and my wish is that this story inspires you to seek until you find. I invite you to tell me what you think.

NOTES

CHAPTER 2   WHAT IS GOD?

1. Frank Sheed, *Theology and Sanity* (San Francisco: Ignatius Press, 1993), 25.
2. Ernest Holmes, *The Science of Mind* (New York: Penguin Putnam, Inc., 1998), 131.

CHAPTER 4   WHAT IS RELIGION?

1. Huston Smith, *The World's Religions* (San Francisco: HarperSanFrancisco, 1991), 60.

CHAPTER 6   WHAT IS CHRISTIANITY?

1. Bart D. Ehrman, *Jesus, Interrupted* (San Francisco: HarperOne, 2009), 1.
2. *Catechism of the Catholic Church* (Washington: United States Catholic Conference, 1994), 106.
3. Ehrman, *Jesus, Interrupted*, 184.

CHAPTER 7   THE DEAL

1. Mt 16:18 (Jerusalem Bible).
2. Jn 3:3–7 (JB).

CHAPTER 8   WHAT IS THE TRINITY?

1. Athanasian Creed.
2. *Catechism*, 253.
3. Jn 14:12, 16–19 (JB).
4. Mt 28:19–20 (JB).

CHAPTER 10   WHO ARE THE CLERGY?

1. *Catechism*, 1578.
2. *Catechism*, 1577.
3. *Catechism*, 1578.
4. Lk 8:1–3 (JB).
5. Lk 10:40–42 (JB).
6. Jn 4:24 (JB).

7. Jn 4:27–28 (JB).
8. Mt 28:10 (JB).
9. Jn 20:17–18 (JB).
10. Karen L. King, *The Gospel of Mary of Magdala* (Santa Rosa, CA: Polebridge Press, 2003), 17.
11. Gal 3:27–28 (JB).
12. Thomas Aquinas, *Summa Theologica,* trans. Fathers of the English Dominican Province (London: Burns, Oates & Washbourne, 1920), 3.31.4.
13. Mt 19:11–12 (JB).
14. Gen 22:17 (JB).
15. Gen 30:23 (JB).

CHAPTER 12   WHO IS JESUS?

1. Lk 17:21 (JB).
2. *Catechism,* 464.
3. Mt 26:64 (JB).
4. Mk 14:61 (JB).
5. Lk 22:70 (JB).
6. Lk 10:22 (JB).
7. Mt 11:27 (JB).
8. Eric Butterworth, *Discover the Power Within You* (San Francisco: HarperSanFrancisco, 1992), 10.
9. Butterworth, *Discover the Power Within You,* 11.
10. Rev 22:16 (JB).
11. Butterworth, *Discover the Power Within You,* 10.
12. Jn 14:10–12 (JB).
13. *Catechism,* 645.
14. Jn 20:26 (JB).

CHAPTER 13   DISCERNING THE DIVINE

1. Elaine Pagels, *Beyond Belief: The Secret Gospel of Thomas* (New York: Vintage, 2003), 227.
2. Alan Jacobs, *The Essential Gnostic Gospels* (London: Watkins Publishing, 2006), 42–43.
3. Jacobs, *The Essential Gnostic Gospels,* 20.

CHAPTER 14   PRACTICING ONENESS

1. *Catechism,* 2559 (quoting Saint John Damascene).
2. Mt 6:5–6 (JB).
3. Butterworth, *Discover the Power Within You,* 106.
4. Jn 4:24 (JB).
5. *Catechism,* 2567.
6. Mt 6:7–9 (JB).
7. Lk 11:9–13 (JB).

TIM O'DONNELL owned and ran a daily newspaper publishing company and won dozens of newspaper publishing awards for excellence. He has also been an organizational consultant, university lecturer, and keynote speaker. In addition, he has led workshops and seminars on leadership and personal and organizational development. His unquenchable curiosity and continuing thirst for asking life's big questions now keep him busy writing, blogging, speaking, and engaging others in meaningful dialogue.

Tim and his wife, Lynn, make their home in Kansas City and have three children. To learn more about Tim O'Donnell and his work, visit www .AViewFromTheBackPew.com, where you can also find more resources for your journey of discovery and join the conversation.